£6.95.

# Secretaries, Management and Organizations

*Susan Vinnicombe*

## Heinemann Educational Books
London

*Heinemann Educational Books Ltd*
*22 Bedford Square, London WC1B 3HH*

LONDON EDINBURGH MELBOURNE AUCKLAND
HONG KONG SINGAPORE KUALA LUMPUR NEW DELHI
IBADAN NAIROBI JOHANNESBURG
EXETER (NH) KINGSTON PORT OF SPAIN


ISBN 0 435 82896 7
© Susan Vinnicombe 1980
First published 1980
Reprinted 1982

| *British Library Cataloguing in Publication Data* |
| --- |
| Vinnicombe, Susan<br>  Secretaries, management and organizations<br>  1. Secretaries   2. Organization<br>  I. Title<br>  658' .3741        HF5547.5<br><br>  ISBN 0-435-82896-7<br><br>*Library of Congress No* 80-670216 |

Typeset by Red Lion Setters, Holborn, London
and Printed in Great Britain by
Richard Clay (The Chaucer Press) Ltd
Bungay, Suffolk

# Contents

# Acknowledgements

This book is based largely on my doctoral thesis completed in 1978 at Manchester Business School. In order to convert the material into an easily readable form I have considerably compressed the analysis of the background literature on secretaries, and I have incorporated only a summary of the research methodology for those who are interested in the approach adopted in the empirical study.

Since this book derives from my thesis I would like to acknowledge the significant contributions of both my supervisors, Professors John Morris and David Weir. The research was financially supported by the Social Science Research Council, the Centre for Business Research at Manchester Business School, and Delta Metal. While I am unable to divulge the names of secretaries and organizations taking part in the research, I would like to record my thanks to them all for generously giving me their time and, in so doing, making this book possible. Fortunately, I am able to thank Yvonne Maidment personally for typing the script so beautifully and so speedily.

Throughout my acknowledgements it is possible to identify different individuals with the specific forms of help they have given me. There is, however, one person who has continually given me all forms of support, and that is Dr David Frankel. Among his many contributions, he has helped me shape my ideas, obtain access to companies, and has painstakingly read this book at every stage of its development. It is with very deep and warm feelings of appreciation that I would like to thank him.

Throughout this book references to a secretary are made in the feminine and references to a boss/manager are made in the masculine. The reasons are twofold. One is to avoid clumsiness in style. Secondly, this reflects the situation in my own study, although in managerial roles such sex-based role differentiations are beginning to become outmoded.

# Introduction

The idea of analysing the role of secretaries in organizations came primarily from two sources: my involvement with them in previous jobs, and the noticeable absence of any reference to them in the management literature. In both these areas it was evident that there was an ignorance surrounding secretarial work and personnel. That this situation continues to exist is surprising since the productivity of organizations is inextricably bound up with the efficient utilization of the secretarial staff. In many important respects they function as the support system within organizations. Most managers recognize the valuable contributions made by their secretaries, yet few initiatives are taken by them to try and understand the potential contributions secretaries could make. There appears to be an implicit assumption among managers that they will automatically know how to work most effectively with their secretaries. Not all the blame lies with individual managers; it is rare for a management training programme to consider the subject. In such an organizational climate it is not surprising that high secretarial turnover, low secretarial efficiency, and low job satisfaction frequently exist.

The need to understand the secretary's role has never been more urgent than now. Today we are entering the age of the word processing system — destined to revolutionize the office over the next decade. Basically, the word processing system is capable of automating every stage in the cycle of producing business documents — from dictation right through to the actual distribution. The concept 'word processing' came from the prediction that word processing would do to office paperwork what data processing has done for the accumulation of numerical data. Clearly, there are tremendous cost and time attractions in implementing word processing systems. Their successful use, however, relies crucially on management's awareness of how the secretary's role within the organization will have to change.

Extensive experience of word processing units in the United States indicates that they can be used in one of two ways. Under both systems is the basic element of splitting the administrative and correspondence functions of the secretary. Word processing may be introduced solely to replace secretarial staff with machines in order to increase speed and quality, and decrease costs. Typically, managers will telephone in their typing to local or central word processing units, where they have no personal relationship with the typists. Some managers will lose their secretaries. Where this kind of system operates there is frequently low user satisfaction, conflict over work priorities, greater burdens placed on managers to check their work, and decreased job satisfaction among the remaining secretaries, since they feel their jobs have been de-enriched.

Instead of using word processing units to replace existing secretarial capacities it can be used to increase and expand the scope of secretarial and managerial staff. This is the imaginative way of capitalizing on the benefits of word processing. When used in this way word processing units are carefully designed at local centres within the organization in order to ensure a close personal relationship between typists and users. The typists will be individuals who are highly skilled both in typing and the nature of the work being undertaken, such that they will be able to do proofing themselves. Under this system, instead of using the secretarial slack to reduce the number of secretaries, it is used to take over many of the lower-order managerial tasks, thus freeing managers to spend more time on high priority tasks. Where word processing has been implemented in this way there has been higher user satisfaction, low conflict over work priorities, high job satisfaction among typists and secretaries, and much higher productivity from the managers. The financial savings have been spectacular. It is worth noting that not all these effects are the direct results of introducing word processing units, but their introduction has acted as an important catalyst in rethinking the role of secretaries in the organization.

If organizations want to benefit from such wide-ranging direct and indirect benefits of word processing units, then there is an urgent need to diagnose real secretarial needs. As a starting-point it is necessary to understand the roles secretaries currently play in organizations and the ways in which they experience their life at work. This book sets out to aid that process of understanding. Initially, the book looks at how secretaries, as a system of workers, fit into organizations. Then it goes on to focus on the activities of top private secretaries, and in particular, the discretionary (administrative) aspects of the private secretary's role.

# 1 | The Development of the Secretarial Role

Although the position of the secretary is commonly observed in almost all organizations, there has been little systematic attempt to understand it. Secretaries never appear on organizational charts and rarely have standard job descriptions. They have been variously referred to as 'the obscure members of the organization'[1] and as 'organizational isolates'.[2]

This traditional lack of formal recognition of secretaries within organizations clearly does not reflect the reality of managerial life. The extent to which organizations need secretaries becomes strikingly evident when they are unexpectedly absent and all their 'hidden' contributions suddenly surface. It is a truism that managers do not miss secretaries until they do not have them, and even then they have some difficulty in identifying precisely what they miss about them. Put more cynically, organizations provide their managers with secretaries as they do cars. Yet more time is spent by managers and organizations scrutinizing and analysing the purchase, allocation, maintenance, and expense of cars, than considering the function, selection, performance, and development of secretaries. And some managers, on joining a new company, are more interested in the car scheme available than the secretarial backing provided.

The need to understand what secretaries can contribute to organizations has become all the more pressing recently with the introduction of word processing units. If companies want to assess the viability of implementing such hardware with the dual goals of increasing secretarial effectiveness and covering secretarial overheads, they must first have a good grasp of what their secretarial needs are and how the latter are or are not currently being met. It is all too easy for management to be infatuated with the capabilities of word processing units, without realizing that their premature introduction may only serve to aggravate their secretarial problems.

The immediate large-scale financial investment surrounding secretarial hardware is an obvious one. Far more inconspicuous and more difficult to manage are the human costs which accompany word processing units. Many managers will have to forfeit their right to a personal secretary — a highly prized symbol of success in their organizational careers. Managers, as a whole, will have to be educated into channelling their typing into a central unit via dictators; bearing in mind the persistent reluctance today of many managers to use dictation machines, this move should not be underestimated. During the initial stages of implementation, at least, there will be secretarial 'slack' in the system since many secretaries will have lost their basic tasks. How this precious time is to be filled is crucial to the over-all effectiveness of the secretarial function. Judging from the many reports and surveys which have highlighted how secretaries are under-utilized today, this situation does not bode well for the word processing age of organizations.

Finally, there are the significant repercussions of word processing units to the structure of the secretarial hierarchy and the design of secretaries' jobs. It is possible that the traditional secretarial hierarchy — pool typist to group secretary to private secretary — is going to split into two distinct halves: those who work in the word processing units and those who work as private secretaries or personal assistants to senior managers. Opinions on this revised structure vary; some see it as a dead end leading to an automated ghetto, while others see word processing as a career ladder into a key managerial position. Certainly the opportunity for individuals to progress gradually up the secretarial hierarchy will disappear. This, then, has profound consequences for the training, selection, and development of secretaries.

What this brief glance at how word processing units might change organizations does highlight, is the fact that managers can no longer afford to ignore the question of secretarial efficiency. They must ask themselves what do their secretaries do and what can be done to ensure that the manager-secretary relationship can operate as effectively as possible. It was with this in mind that this book was written. It sets out to explore how secretaries fit into organizations; specifically it focuses on what secretaries do in their jobs, how they see themselves, and how effective they can be to their managers. Ultimately this book attempts to provide some guidance for helping organizations — the managers, secretaries, personnel, and training functions within them — to improve both the job satisfaction and efficiency of secretaries.

Before looking at how the secretarial role has been portrayed in the organizational and management literature, it is useful as an introduction to highlight three important historical factors which have influenced the development of the secretarial function. They are the growth of white-collar work in Great Britain, the development of the bureaucracy, and the role of women in the office.

## Growth of white-collar work

The enormous expansion of office jobs in the whole occupational spectrum must constitute one of the overriding characteristics of modern industrial societies. The growth of white-collar employees is both absolute and relative; not only is the number of white-collar workers increasing, but so also is the proportion of these workers in the labour force as a whole. Between 1911 and 1971 the number of white-collar employees increased by 203 per cent, while the comparable number for manual workers was a decline of 2 per cent. The discrepant growth of these two groups can be seen in the increasing relative importance of the white-collar occupations. The white-collar section of the labour force increased from 18.7 per cent to 42.7 per cent of the total between 1911 and 1971 while the manual share decreased from 74.6 per cent to 54.7 per cent.[3] 'These changes which occur in all industrial societies have been slow and almost imperceptible, but their cumulative effects allow one to speak of a veritable administrative revolution of the twentieth century.'[4]

It is extremely difficult to define white-collar workers along any single dimension of stratification — skills, functions, class, status, or power. Perhaps a major reason for this is that 'white collar people do not complete one compact horizontal stratum'.[5] In an in-depth analysis of definitions of white-collar workers, however, it has been suggested that it is possible to thread together the various conclusions on the subject. The authors propose that the features which are normally identified as distinguishing white-collar workers — type of dress, the nature of the work environment, and the functions performed — can all be regarded as different external symbols of a more fundamental common feature: the possession of, or proximity to, authority. Thus although most white-collar employees occupy subordinate positions in the organization in the same way as blue-collar employees, they are associated 'with the part of the production process where authority is exercised and decisions taken'.[6] This conclusion is especially relevant to a discussion of secretaries, since their role essentially derives from their managers in the organization, who hold positions of authority and are traditionally associated with the process of decision-making.

Despite the differences in cultural backgrounds to their white-collar studies, Mills[7] and Lockwood[8] tend to agree on the main factors accounting for the development of white-collar workers. The first was that the market from which clerical workers were recruited was expanded enormously by the extension of compulsory elementary education in the last decades of the nineteenth century. Any person who was literate became a potential clerk. This situation radically ousted the existing prestigious position then held by the 'blackcoated' worker.

The second factor was increased productivity gained from the continually improved machinery used in production processes. As machinery became more sophisticated so it became inevitable that unskilled workers were displaced, making craft skills unnecessary and, in consequence, increasing the importance of the machine operator. From then onwards workers comprising the new lower classes tended to be predominantly semi-skilled.

The proliferation of the non-productive commercial functions, like transportation and finance, occurred because a greater proportion of the labour force was required in the distribution of the products that resulted from increased production. Mills hypothesized that this shift reflected the central problem of modern industrial structure, that is, the need to find and create markets. These last two factors can be illustrated with some figures on the breakdown of white-collar employment. Over the period 1951 to 1971 the number of white-collar employees in Great Britain rose from 5.74 to 8.88 million. Fifty-eight per cent of the 3.14 million rise occurred from the growth in total employment within certain industrial sectors (a shift away from the primary, and to a lesser extent, from the secondary sector, to the tertiary sector). The remaining 42 per cent growth in white-collar employment resulted from the changing occupational structure within industries, whereby increasing numbers of white-collar workers were being substituted for blue-collar workers.[9] The phenomenal increase in white-collar workers in the British economy thus reflected not only a shift in employment between the industrial sectors, but also a shift in employment within each sector. This leads into the fourth factor affecting the development of white-collar work — which will be taken up in the next section — the rise of 'big business'.

## The development of the bureaucracy

The term 'bureaucracy' has been defined in a number of ways, ranging from a large-scale organization with specialized functions,[10] to the administrative subsystem of an organization,[11] to being merely a characteristic of an organization's functioning.[12] (Thus one speaks of an organization as being 'very' or 'not very bureaucratic'.) While it is difficult to isolate one single definition it is less problematic to identify the typical characteristics of bureaucracy.

These are as follows:
1 Hierarchy of authority.
2 Division of labour.
3 Formal work procedures.
4 Extensive rules.
5 Limited authority of organizational position.
6 Differential rewards by organizational position.
7 Rational discipline.
8 Impersonality of personal contact.
9 Administration separate from management/ownership.
10 Emphasis on written communication.[13]

The last three characteristics listed are particularly important in tracing the role of secretaries in organizations, because it was the increased complexity of communication and co-ordination associated with having large numbers of staff that led to the need for a substantive administrative component in organizations.

There are two main contrasting views on explaining how the size of the administrative component develops relative to the size of organizations. One suggests that it decreases with increased organizational size,[14] while the converse and popular view held by Parkinson is that it increases with increased size.[15] One of the problems in reconciling these views comes back to definitions again, in particular of deciding where the administrative component begins and ends in an organization. In an interesting piece of research two aspects of the administrative system of the organization — the managerial and the clerical staff — are singled out, and distinguished in terms of the types of co-ordinative functions they perform. The managerial personnel correspond to the decision-makers and co-ordinators of subordinates, while the clerical personnel are concerned mainly with the flow of information in the organization. The author suggests that his results concerning the dynamics of bureaucratic administration point to a 'functional equivalence' hypothesis. That is, with greater organizational size, clerical personnel increasingly replace managerial personnel in co-ordinative functions.[16]

This transferral of communication and co-ordination from management to clerical staff may be explained in terms of efficiency. That is, it is less costly to delegate such functions than for management to carry them out themselves. It may also, however, be closely linked to the increasing professionalism of managers that has made them disparage the administrative activities necessitated by their jobs. Another reason may be quite simply that managers are under increasing amounts of pressure in their jobs, such that they no longer have the time to take responsibility for these activities. However, Tracy is more cynical.[17] He specifically identifies secretaries within the clerical component, and suggests that they form a completely separate and distinct element in the organization structure which he calls a 'para-hierarchy' of administrative talent. (He defines a para-hierarchy as a grouping of people in positions parallel to a hierarchy.) Similarly, Korda sees secretaries operating in a separate hierarchy to management; he refers to them as 'alternative management' and gives several vivid examples of how they can effectively function on behalf of their managers as sounding-boards for ideas, and as barometers of the organizational climate.[18] This would certainly explain secretaries' absence from traditional organizational charts. Further, Tracy posits that organizations' survival is due in large part to these secretaries who increasingly compensate for their bosses the further they are up the hierarchy. He calls this the Productive Para-hierarchy Principle: 'In order to survive a dominant hierarchy must create and maintain a para-hierarchy composed of members of a subordinate class to whom the Peter Principle does not apply.'[19]

## The role of women in the office

It is against this background to the development of the administrative side of the organization that perhaps the most perceptible symptom of the 'white-collar revolution' must be examined. This is the part played by the white-collar woman. Female clerks, as a percentage of total clerks, have spiralled from 0.1 per cent in 1851 to 72 per cent in 1971. The percentage of workers employed as clerks rose far more strikingly for women than for men, and so, as Lockwood suggests, it is much more accurate to speak of the 'white bloused worker' than the 'white-collar worker'.[20] The interesting point here is the background of the women attracted into the occupation. While women in manual work are still recruited from working-class families, and women in the professions come mainly from middle- and upper-class families, the two seem to meet in routine non-manual work as typists and secretaries.[21] This is probably one of the main reasons why secretarial work has acquired the image of being 'a nice job for a girl'. There are other obvious attractions to it. It is a clean and respectable job, it does not require unsocial hours, it is comparatively well paid, and there is relatively easy entry. In addition, it is one of the few occupations for which one can acquire the basic skills at school.

It might be thought, then, that the development of white-collar work opened up the job market for women, offering some the opportunity to improve their class position in society. An analysis of women's earnings relative to men, however, indicates that there has been, and still is, tremendous monetary sex inequality. Among clerks, the average earnings for women relative to the average earnings for men in 1922-4 was 57 per cent and only increased by 2 per cent to 59 per cent in 1960.[22]

While it is not possible to relate the earnings of female secretaries and typists to male secretaries and typists, since the number of the latter is negligible, it can still be concluded that there is a large gap between men's and women's earnings within the clerical structure over all. In fact, the very absence of males as secretaries and typists (see Table 1.1) may be partly attributed to the lack of attraction of secretarial work in terms of financial earnings (particularly in comparison to what males can earn elsewhere), and to employers who have always projected the image of secretarial work as being female.

Table 1.1    *Growth of typists, shorthand writers and secretaries*

|      | Total   | Number of males | % of total | Number of females | % of total |
|------|---------|-----------------|------------|-------------------|------------|
| 1951 | 510 337 | 15 346          | 3.0        | 494 991           | 97         |
| 1961 | 663 960 | 13 940          | 2.1        | 650 020           | 97.9       |
| 1966 | 803 520 | 14 620          | 1.8        | 788 900           | 98.2       |
| 1971 | 747 400 | 10 100          | 1.4        | 737 800           | 98.6       |

*Source:*   Census, England and Wales, Occupational Tables, 1951, 1961, 1971.
Sample Census, Great Britain, Economic Activity Tables, 1966. Office of Population Censuses and Surveys (H.M.S.O.).

The reasons for the latter situation are complex, and are certainly bound up with the notion of the secretary being a status symbol for the boss, and on purely financial grounds employers could confidently assume that female secretaries would be less liable to push for higher earnings than their male counterparts. This in turn relates to women's perceptions of work and their attitudes to trade unions. Only 6 per cent of secretaries in Great Britain belong to trade unions[23] and the only sign of any militancy among secretaries in this country was the march by a number of Civil Service secretaries in 1974 over the issue of pay in relation to full-time and temporary secretaries.

The introduction of the typewriter in 1875 in Great Britain marked the advent of women's entry into the office. In time a standard female hierarchy evolved in offices, based on a taxonomy of skills allied to the typewriter. At the bottom is the pool typist and at the top the white-collar stereotype — the personal secretary — whose duty it is to 'identify herself completely with her employer's interest and minister to his comforts and peace of mind'.[24] She is frequently referred to as 'the office wife'.[25]

The metaphor of the 'office wife' is apt since the private secretary emerges as much as the boss's primary partner, support, and confidante in the work context, as does the wife in the home environment. Further, it is not unknown for the private secretary to be more in touch with the boss's activities, both on a work and private front, than the wife. In some situations she may even be called upon to protect the boss from his wife! Kanter, in her book *Men and Women of the Corporation* elaborates on the appropriateness of the marriage metaphor:

> ... choice of a secretary on the basis of personal qualities like appearance, fusion of the couple in the eyes of others, a non-rationalized relationship with terms set by personal negotiation; expectations of personal service, including office 'house-work' — special understandings that do not survive the particular relationship; expectations of personal loyalty and symbolic or emotional rewards — and an emotional division of labour in which the woman plays the emotional role and the man the providing role. Indeed, the progression from the secretarial pool and multiple bosses to a position working for just one manager resembles the progression from dating to marriage.[26]

The importance of identifying the sexist side to the secretarial role is important, because just as the majority of secretaries are female (99 per cent)[27] so the majority of their bosses are male (83 per cent).[28] (The last figure is actually much greater than this since administrators are amalgamated with managers in this classification.) In fact, the secretarial and managerial roles probably represent the most sex segregated roles in the whole organization. It is essential to be aware of this in appreciating how the working relationship has developed.

## A brief overview of the secretarial role

The secretary's job has a long history, for until relatively recently, the skill of writing was possessed by only a few people. The word 'secretary' derives from the Latin *secretum*, and in medieval times a secretary was the person who dealt with the correspondence of the king, or other high-ranking person, and consequently with confidential and secret matters.[29] Although a variety of tasks are associated with the secretary today, the original notions of confidentiality and skill in correspondence are still the elements most traditionally linked with the occupation.

While shorthand and typing skills are essential to the position of a private/personal secretary, they may, by no means, be the clerical skills exploited by the employer. Fiore elaborates on this point. He suggests that the activities of the private secretary may be perceived from a dual functionalist perspective. There are those allied to word processing which Fiore regards as 'mechanistic' in nature, and those allied to general administration which he regards as 'organic' in nature (see Table 1.2).[30]

Table 1.2   *Functional characteristics of the secretary's position*

| Mechanistic (typing activities) | Organic (administration/non-typing activities) |
|---|---|
| 1 Job description easier | 1 Job description more difficult |
| 2 Input/output more controllable | 2 Input/output less controllable |
| 3 Problems more predictable | 3 Problems less predictable |
| 4 Task elements largely psychometric | 4 Task elements largely cognitive |
| 5 Independent activity more vital to productivity | 5 Dynamic interaction more vital to productivity |
| 6 Creativity/innovation areas circumscribed | 6 Creativity/innovation areas less circumscribed |
| 7 Development more visible | 7 Development less visible |
| 8 Peer competition visible | 8 Peer competition less visible |
| 9 Multi-channel communication less essential to effectiveness | 9 Multi-channel communication more essential to effectiveness |
| 10 Success relatively independent of particular boss supported | 10 Success relatively dependent on particular boss supported |

*Source:*   Fiore, M., 'The Secretarial Role in Transition', *Supervisory Management*, November 1971, p. 22.

The distinction between mechanistic and organic activities is best brought out by relating them to specific secretarial jobs. At one end of the scale is the pool typist. She works alongside other pool typists and her work consists wholly of copy typing, which has been given to her by a number of junior managers, or allocated to her by a pool supervisor. Her job is thus totally routine with immediate visible results which are easily measured. Her success is entirely dependent on her speed and accuracy of typing and thus communication with other people is not only unimportant but in most cases is disruptive to performance. Even work originators tend not to brief her personally on the typing; they will merely leave her some written instructions. The pool typist characterizes a secretarial position where activities are wholly mechanistic.

At the other end of the scale is the senior executive secretary or personal assistant to the managing director. She may spend little or no time typing since she may have her own junior secretary to whom such tasks can be delegated. Instead, most of her day is spent in a supportive administrative capacity carrying out a variety of tasks, from making the coffee to taking her boss's place at a meeting. This kind of secretary works very closely with her boss, and indeed, her success depends vitally on maintaining this co-ordinated team approach. The personal secretary not only undertakes anything required of her by her boss but also, and importantly, initiates many work-based activities herself.

Again, the effectiveness with which she carries out the latter depends on how well she knows her boss and can anticipate his needs. Often such secretaries have spent many years, in some cases a working lifetime, with one boss. Such secretaries frequently pride themselves on being able to predict precisely what the boss's reaction is going to be in any given situation. It is not surprising that they are often used as the boss's barometer in decision-making. Whereas in the situation of the pool typist it is easy to control work and measure performance, with the personal secretary work-loads are contingent on the boss's work-loads, and performance is difficult to gauge since outcomes are not always immediate or quantifiable. Also, the pool typist may be very successful in terms of carrying out her duties, in adopting a very calculated interest in her work, illustrated by, for example, strictly adhering to office hours. This would be a formula for failure with the personal secretary who, unless she is prepared to work late and take jobs home with her, would never be successful. She has to let her work demands define her day. Such a private secretary occupies a secretarial position where activities are largely organic.

Needless to say, the above two descriptions typify opposite ends on a continuum defining a secretary's position. Once an individual is no longer a pool typist it becomes difficult to define her job accurately, since it tends to be a blend of mechanistic and organic activities. The relative proportions which make up any one secretary's job are primarily determined by her boss, with the secretary bringing to bear a certain amount of influence. The nature of the boss's position and the industry in which he is located will also affect this situation. These external factors will be taken up for discussion in Chapter 3.

If the personal/executive secretary stands at the 'top' of the female hierarchy in the office, in between her and the pool typist is the departmental or group secretary (sometimes referred to as a short-hand typist). They possess both typing and shorthand skills, like the top secretaries, but rather than working exclusively for one boss they tend to work for a group of managers. Thus they are unable to build up the same degree of personal identification with a boss as the personal secretaries, and they are likely to undertake less administrative duties than do personal secretaries. It is quite common for group secretaries, for instance, neither to take bosses' telephone calls nor to control their diaries.

The secretarial hierarchy may be defined along a number of general characteristics common to any other organization's hierarchy, e.g. status, salary, size of office, autonomy. What particularly distinguishes movement up the secretarial hierarchy, however, may be reduced to two factors:

1 The degree to which the boss-secretary relationship becomes personalized.
2 The degree to which the dependency relationship between boss(es) and secretary shifts from being one where the secretary is totally dependent on her boss(es) to one where the boss becomes almost totally dependent on the secretary.

The second factor needs some elaboration. At the bottom of the hierarchy the typist relies totally on the boss to determine her work-load, define her activities, and check her work, whereas at the top of the organization it is the secretary who plays a significant and visible role determining her boss's work-load, defining his activities, and checking that he has completed all his tasks (see Figure 1.1). The nature of the dependency relationship has thus effectively been totally reversed. On the whole, the degree to which the boss-secretary relationship becomes personalized and the dependency relationship alters are not independent; generally, secretaries who work closer with their bosses and identify with them are the ones whose bosses rely on them totally in order to carry out their jobs effectively.

Recent developments in the structure of offices have probably tended to widen the differences between the three levels of this hierarchy. There is a tendency to 'pool' typists and shorthand typists together in order to increase the efficiency of the service. One advertising and marketing company in London estimated a saving of

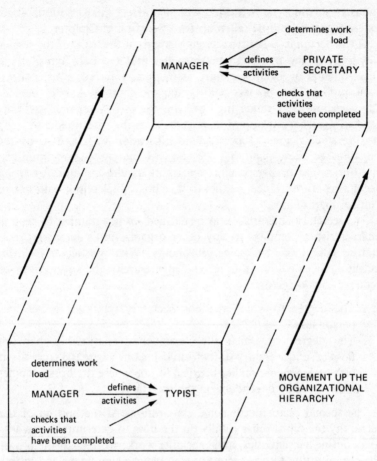

**Fig 1.1**   *Secretarial movement up the organizational hierarchy*

£17,000 a year through adopting a centralized dictating system in the office.[31] The consequences of this move are that the skill of short-hand is becoming obsolete (having been replaced by dictation machines); the tasks have become more routinized; and the white-collar woman in this situation has become easily replaceable. The widespread implementation of word processing units will exacerbate this gap. Within this context it is easy to see why the occupation has been able to accommodate part-time temporary staff. The new white-collar woman operating as a typist or word processing operator is no longer able to develop expertise in one area of the business, and she has lost the close contact which she previously had with management; in this respect her status has been seriously impoverished. A possible result of these changes occurring at the bottom of the female white-collar hierarchy is that it has inflated the prestige attributed to the position of private secretary. Within the latter position itself, as a result of the introduction of automated equipment into the office, there will probably be a shift towards greater emphasis on the activities allied to what Fiore calls the 'organic' function. In this respect private secretaries may act more as 'personal assistants' than as mere typists.[32]

The secretarial hierarchy is relatively short in terms of how long it takes to work from the bottom to the top. It is much more common to see top secretaries in their late thirties or early forties than it is to see their equivalent managing directors of the same age. Having said that, it does not follow that promotion comes quickly or easily. Initially, promotion for a secretary is almost completely dependent on individual members of the managerial hierarchy 'spotting' potential in the typing pool or department. The individual then becomes a personal secretary and further promotion up the organization usually depends upon the boss's promotion. In other words, bosses opt as to whether or not to carry their secretaries up the hierarchy with them. It is also worth highlighting the organizational practice whereby managers are deemed to need personal secretaries in the first place. This is not linked to any formal rational analysis of work-load, but rather when a manager reaches a certain status level in the organization, usually senior manager level, he is automatically given a secretary. Private secretaries are thus often perceived as perks or rewards for performance. In this respect private secretaries operate as symbols of success and prestige for their respective managers.

The nature of a secretary's promotion up the organization reinforces the appropriateness of the reference to her as the 'office wife'. Like the boss's wife who may assume her social status via her husband, so at work the secretary acquires her position and status through her boss. On account of the lack of any standard job descriptions, rational criteria for allocating secretaries, or performance appraisal schemes for secretaries, the latter are often in a relatively powerless position to manipulate their careers. It is paradoxical that while the secretarial position came through the bureaucratization of organizations, it goes contrary to all the principles of bureaucracy: namely, rationality, depersonalization of relationships, and the application of universal standards. The boss-secretary relationship represents the most striking example of the retention of patrimony within the organization.[33]

One of the key contributions perceived of private secretaries is the way they operate as a 'system of cliques' within and between formal lines of authority, thus facilitating the handling of issues which might have taken much longer had they gone through the regular channels of communication. Eccles suggests that the importance of the secretary in handling issues on the boss's behalf is particularly pronounced when the boss is working on assignments away from the home office. He suggests that secretaries act as 'interpreters, guides, fixers, filters, negotiators and organisers of the debates about important problems'.[34] The relationship between boss and private secretary is, then, necessarily a supportive one and one in which there is a reciprocation of influence and prestige. Roman elaborates on this point: 'A secretary ... is a skilled executive and interpreter of her boss's thinking and she is often the executant of their thinking, especially so in the absence of the boss'.[35]

There may, however, be certain problems. Bensaher highlights a critical one which deserves far more attention than it receives. Since the secretary so frequently acts as the boss's surrogate/substitute, it is essential that the boss and secretary have some 'mutually agreed framework within which she is to operate'. If this framework is not worked out it is possible that the secretary is not acting within the interests of the boss.[36] This point relates to the fact that the boss and private secretary must think, plan, and act as a team. Just as the success of a doubles partnership in tennis critically depends on the ability of each player to anticipate the shots of the other, to complement one another's style and to synchronize their game, so also the boss and private secretary should work hard at developing their team strategy. In this respect it is a great shame that management and secretarial training programmes persist in training the partners separately, thus reinforcing this rift.

In conclusion, then, the importance of the private secretarial role lies in its symbiotic relationship to its parallel managerial position. This manifests itself in two ways. First, a high status is conferred on the private secretary through her close working relationship with her boss. Secondly, and this is the one which forms the focus of this book, an important function is fulfilled by the private secretary in terms of the way she acts as an 'extension' to her boss, and on occasions even as a surrogate to him.

The executive has turned his secretary into his gatekeeper. She can filter, certainly deter, maybe veto the importunings of the would-be visitors. Is there any reader who doesn't know of situations where it is more important to be well-in with the secretary than with the executive himself? Are there no cases where the enquirer gets better, more useful, information from the secretary? The gatekeeper secretary is performing a managerial function. The executive depends on her for the receipt of authentic information. She is adjacent to the circulation of people in the corridor and may well see more of them than he does. In his absence she has to take decisions for him. She may have much greater contact with the day to day network in the organisation.[37]

The importance of the gatekeeper role of the personal secretary has been demonstrated in a large organizational communications study in Florida. In the project the researchers analysed the frequency with which individuals communicated with other individuals; the direction of the communications (i.e. who initiated contact); and the nature of the communications. The results indicated that it was one of the director's secretaries who had greatest access to information, and information sources, in the company. What is especially interesting here is that a top secretary not only emerged as a more important liaison than other lower-level secretaries, but that she was more important than all the directors.[38] This must rank as a critical observation in appreciating how organization communication systems really work. With this in mind it is not surprising that Sorensen sums up the private secretarial position in these terms: 'the key member of the manager's team should be his secretary',[39] and MacKenzie states: 'Of the many resources contributing to the manager's effectiveness, none is more critical than his secretary'.[40]

# 2 | The Organizational Context to Secretarial Work

In order to understand what any one secretary does in her job, it is necessary to appreciate first the over-all organizational context within which secretaries operate. The case study which forms the basis of this chapter derives from an in-depth analysis of a large professional service company in London. The research was undertaken in 1975.

The data were collected by means of a series of interviews with members of management, group discussions with all the secretarial staff, and diary analyses, in which all the secretaries recorded their activities over a period of two weeks. The company described in the case study was not selected in order to illustrate the effective or ineffective use of secretaries; rather, the research was part of a much bigger project which the company management had introduced in order to improve the efficiency with which they employed their secretaries. The very fact that they initiated the study shows a certain sensitivity to secretarial utilization which is rarely displayed in organizations. As such, the problems and issues that emerge in the case study are by no means unique to this company. Indeed it would be extremely unlikely if the reader could not identify any of them in his/her own organization.

## The organization setting

Figures was a large reputable company operating in the City, which offered professional advice in a number of fields, including financial management. In 1975 there were 143 secretarial staff in Figures, of which 124 were permanent and the rest temporary. They were located in three buildings in the City, two quite close to one another and the other about half a mile away. This geographical break-up meant that secretaries tended to know only the secretaries in their own building, rather than the secretaries who worked in any of the other buildings.

The whole subject of location and accommodation was a delicate one. In general, space was so scarce that secretaries shared offices. Usually there were two to six in each office. The only exception to this rule were the top six private secretaries who worked exclusively for the directors of the company. They had small offices to themselves. Also, it was not always possible to locate secretaries' offices next to their bosses. The very worst example of this was a secretary who was four floors away from her boss. The other repercussion of this shortage of space was that management did not have any company canteen or rest facilities for its staff. Thus secretaries usually resorted to staying in their offices at lunch-time.

## Background of the secretaries

Figures was divided into six departments, one being devoted to administration and the other five covering varying areas of professional services. In terms of the breakdown of the permanent secretarial staff by age and length of service, the following facts were significant. The largest proportion of the staff was very young; nearly 50 per cent were under the age of 25 and only 11 per cent were aged over 40. In total, the average age was 28. While the average age in the company consistently increased the higher up the hierarchy, the discrepancies between the three were not large; seven years between the top and middle and only one year between the middle and bottom.

In terms of length of service, the largest category of staff (27 per cent) had only between one and six months experience and 64 per cent had had less than two years experience. Only 14 per cent of the secretarial staff had worked for the company for more than five years. Length of service and level in the secretarial hierarchy in the company did not necessarily correspond. While directors' and senior managers' private secretaries had had an average of five years experience in Figures, the middle managers' secretaries had had on average only one and a half years experience compared to the one and three-quarters years of typists (see Table 2.1). This observation was consistent with the point raised in the last chapter, where it was observed that progression up the secretarial hierarchy is a somewhat haphazard process.

The salary system for the secretarial staff was based on age, experience, and merit, hence it was possible for an older person to receive less than a younger one on account of the performance appraisal system. Annual salary increments for both seniority and merit were small, at only £100 each. Thus in theory, the difference between a good and a bad secretary in terms of performance was £100

**Table 2.1  Analysis of length of service as at January 1975 – permanent staff**

| Length of service | Total | % of total | Partners and directors' secretaries | | | | | | | Managers' secretaries | | | | | | | Copy and audio typists | | | | | | |
|---|---|---|---|---|---|---|---|---|---|---|---|---|---|---|---|---|---|---|---|---|---|---|---|
| | | | A | B | C | D | E | F | % | A | B | C | D | E | F | % | A | B | C | D | E | F | % |
| Under 1 month | | | | | | | | | | | | | | | | | | | | | | | |
| 1-6 months | 33 | 27 | 3 | 5 | 1 | 1 | | | 20 | 3 | 5 | 1 | 1 | 1 | 2 | 27 | 1 | 4 | 5 | | | 2 | 42 |
| 7-12 months | 17 | 14 | 1 | 4 | 1 | | | | 12 | 1 | 5 | | | | | 13 | | 3 | 1 | | | | 14 |
| 1-2 years | 29 | 23 | 2 | 5 | 1 | | 1 | 1 | 20 | 1 | 9 | 1 | 1 | 2 | 1 | 33 | 1 | | 2 | | | | 14 |
| 2-3 years | 18 | 15 | 2 | 5 | 1 | | | | 16 | 1 | 5 | 1 | | | | 16 | 2 | | 1 | | 1 | | 10 |
| 3-5 years | 10 | 7 | 1 | 3 | 1 | | | | 10 | | 1 | | | | 1 | 4 | | 3 | | | | | 10 |
| Over 5 years | 17 | 14 | 1 | 6 | 2 | 1 | 1 | | 22 | | 1 | | | | 2 | 7 | 1 | | 2 | | | | 10 |
| *Total* | 124 | 100% | 10 | 28 | 7 | 2 | 2 | 1 | 100 | 6 | 26 | 1 | 2 | 3 | 7 | 100 | 4 | 13 | 9 | | | | 100 |
| Average length of service | 2¾ years | | 5 years | | | | | | | 1½ years | | | | | | | 1¾ years | | | | | | |

in her annual increment (i.e. £100 instead of £200). The forms, however, which were the basis of the performance appraisal system and were supposed to be submitted annually by all managers, were only submitted by about one-third of them. One of the reasons for this was that there was widespread ignorance about the system by both managers and secretaries. Also, where managers did know of the system they could rarely be bothered to apply it, and when they did use the system they often did so without consulting their secretaries. The performance appraisal system, then, was infrequently applied by managers and where it was it operated very ineffectively.

## The secretarial structure

The shape of the secretarial structure was interesting; instead of reflecting the usual tall pyramid shape of traditional managerial hierarchies it was exactly the opposite, being short and top-heavy. In other words, there was a wide band of high status private secretaries at the top which gradually decreased in number towards the middle, where there were group secretaries, and rapidly tapered towards the bottom level of typists. In terms of numbers, the top level consisted of fifty permanent secretarial staff, the middle had forty-five, and the bottom level twenty-nine (see Figure 2.1).

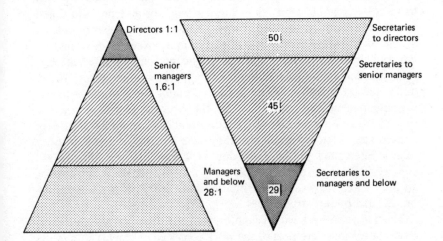

**Fig 2.1**  *The structure of secretaries in Figures*

Complementing this secretarial structure at Figures there was the temporary staff group. At the time of the study this consisted of nineteen, most of whom (thirteen) were concentrated in the middle band. In addition there were ten unfilled posts. Therefore the complete establishment of secretaries accounted for 153.

Directors and senior managers had their own private secretaries. In contrast, middle managers usually headed a set of managers who shared a secretary. She was known as a group secretary on account of this arrangement. These groups varied in size from about six to about twenty managers and assistant managers; sometimes they consisted of a mixture of managers from different areas of specialization. In three departments there were additional copy typists who were structured into 'pools', and they were available to do any work which was routine and could not be handled by the secretaries because of time pressure. The other three departments also had access to copy typing facilities but on a smaller scale.

### The allocation of work

In the one to one working relationship, work was allocated directly by bosses to their private secretaries. The secretaries to groups of managers might check informally on the work position and provide mutual assistance where this was required. In the event of any one group secretary either having too much work or not enough, she was supposed to contact support services which was headed by two females, who would then reallocate her work or give her additional work as the situation required. Copy typing in the pool was organized in one of two ways. Either it was placed in a basket from which the typists helped themselves, starting at the bottom; or alternatively, each job had to be entered on a copy typing request form, which instructed the member of the pool undertaking the work as to the format, spacing, and paper on which the job was to be done, and the time by which it was required. Under normal circumstances tasks were undertaken in the order in which they were received, unless a priority request intervened, in which case that work was done immediately. All copy typing was normally completed within four days. In the case of an impossible work-load the situation was examined by the appropriate head of support services.

The nature of work varied slightly from one department to another. Essentially, however, most of the work consisted of copy typing in the form of routine correspondence, memoranda, accounts, or reports. Since the company prided itself on the quality of its reports, it was not uncommon for them to go through a number of re-typing stages — one famous case was quoted of the report that was typed twenty-two times! There was no formal system of control over secretarial work. On a day-to-day basis complaints were channelled directly to the private secretaries by their respective bosses or to typing pool supervisors, where they existed.

## The secretaries, as perceived by management

Top management's primary concern about the secretaries was their monetary cost. Since they were unable to employ and maintain a full set of permanent secretarial staff, they were forced into the position of using temporary secretaries. This was a situation which is not uncommon in a number of companies and indeed is somewhat seasonal in character, summer being particularly demanding on the temporary secretarial market. Figures Limited, however, felt that they depended upon this facility far more than other companies, and this concerned them considerably since, as they perceived it, the cost of employing a temporary secretary far exceeded that of a permanent one. In addition, the nature of the work at Figures Limited did not really lend itself towards using temporary staff. Figures Limited was a reputable professional service company, thus a large proportion of the secretarial work consisted of typing reports and accounts for clients. The company had evolved a set of routines for the layout of the work which were strictly enforced. Any new employee learned these work procedures informally from the other secretarial staff sharing her office. If she was lucky there might be a work manual available in her office. Basically, however, the success of the system depended upon the other secretaries in the office having the time and willingness to teach the typing layout to the new member. It was felt that it took several days to 'get into it'. Since temporary staff invariably stayed only one week this was a somewhat time-consuming and frustrating task for the permanent secretaries.

Added to these complexities, since Figures Limited was a professional service company the work-load could be uneven, depending on the state of the market. This unevenness manifested itself not only in aggregate terms, i.e. the quantity of work being handled for clients at any one time in the company as a whole, but also in local terms, i.e. the amount of work going through any one group of managers or an individual manager. The latter was a particularly important characteristic of the work situation, since it meant that secretaries could frequently experience slack in their jobs. When this occurred they were expected to use their initiative and 'ask around' for work. Officially they were supposed to telephone support services, whose task it was to recruit and maintain the secretarial staff. This formal system, however, was not effectively used. Normally the permanent secretaries would ask other secretaries in their offices or adjacent offices for extra work, and, conversely, managers also tended to approach specific secretaries personally when they wanted extra work done. The system thus operated on the informal contacts that had developed within the company.

There were several inherent weaknesses in the system. Some secretaries refused to do work for anyone but their immediate bosses. They were often referred to as the *prima donnas* at Figures. Also, since certain secretaries were renowned for being good at their jobs they were frequently overloaded with work during busy times. In contrast, since temporary staff were not in the company long enough to establish such ties of friendship, they were not approached by other secretaries or managers, and consequently were more likely to experience longer periods of total inactivity than the permanent secretaries. Furthermore, management pointed out that temporary staff were frequently seen to be somewhat disruptive to permanent staff, in terms of publicly advertising what they were being paid — which was usually more than their counterparts were receiving — and thus causing friction.

The above reasons, then, made top management very concerned about their degree of reliance upon temporary staff. Trends in the number of secretarial staff and the way the latter broke down into the permanents and temporaries are shown in Figure 2.2. It can be seen

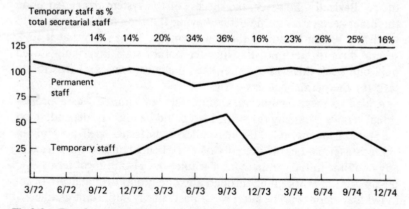

**Fig 2.2**   *Trends in numbers of secretarial staff, 1972-4*

that the two noticeable peaks for temporary secretaries were the two summer seasons charted; September 1973 was particularly pronounced, with the size of the temporary staff reaching 36 per cent of the total secretarial staff. The number of temporary staff employed is directly related to the labour turnover of the permanent staff. As can be seen from Figure 2.2, labour turnover decreased significantly in 1974 compared with the previous two years and concomitantly there were less temporary staff employed.

The statistics for turnover for the years 1972-4 are shown in Table 2.2, together with a breakdown of the various reasons given for

Table 2.2  *Labour turnover amongst the secretarial staff for the period 1972-4*

| Reasons for leaving | 1972 | 1973 | 1974 | Total | % of total |
|---|---|---|---|---|---|
| 1  Marriage/pregnancy | 10 | 13 | 11 | 34 | 18 |
| 2  Ill health | 1 | – | – | 1 | 1 |
| 3  Difficulty of travelling to work | 14 | 12 | 4 | 30 | 16 |
| 4  Husband or self moving from London | 14 | 12 | 9 | 35 | 19 |
| 5  Temporary work or higher salary | 3 | 10 | 2 | 15 | 8 |
| 6  Dissatisfaction with current job | 34 | 21 | 15 | 70 | 38 |
| *Total* | 76 | 68 | 41 | 185 | 100 |
| Labour turnover (as a percentage of total staff) | 65% | 52% | 28% | | |

leaving the company. As can be seen, labour turnover was high among secretarial staff, with 1972 and 1973 reaching over 50 per cent. One of the major contributing factors to the improvement noted in 1974 was thought to be the declining economic climate, which meant that there were less jobs available. Management thus felt that this dampening of high turnover was heavily contingent on the external environment, and that as soon as this improved so the labour turnover would deteriorate again. It is worth highlighting that the largest category recorded the reason for leaving as being 'dissatisfaction with current job'. In other words, it seemed that the intrinsic nature of the job was a prime cause for wanting to leave the company. Although turnover had improved, that in itself was not an index of organizational efficiency. Figures Limited perceived its secretaries as having less job mobility in 1974, and that this was possibly precipitating a situation where dissatisfied secretaries were staying on in their jobs.

## An activity analysis of secretarial jobs

As is evident in Figure 2.3, the split of secretarial activities up the hierarchy is consistent with the description of the secretary's job as discussed in Chapter 1. That is, that a typist's job consists wholly of
typing, and that as a secretary ascends the hierarchy she takes on a
greater variety of tasks allied to the personal assistant aspect of her
role. In Figures, typists spent 74 per cent of their time typing, with no
time spent on other job activities (the rest of the time was spent on
personal tasks or waiting for work); group secretaries spent less time
typing (63.5 per cent), with the remainder of their time distributed
across the other six activities recorded; and the private secretaries
spent 44 per cent of their time typing, thus the greater part of their
working day was taken up with activities outside of typing. All

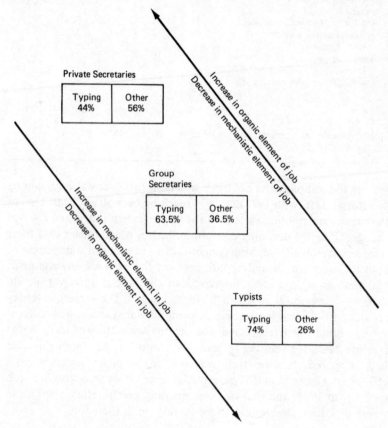

**Fig 2.3** *The profiles of secretaries' jobs*

secretarial staff spent a significant amount of time typing, as a result of the nature of the organization's activities. In other types of organizations, e.g. manufacturing, this changing balance in secretarial activities is likely to be much more pronounced, with private secretaries spending far less time typing.

The breakdown of secretarial activities is shown in detail in Table 2.3. As time spent on typing decreases as one moves up the hierarchy so time taken up with every other activity increases, i.e. dictation,

Table 2.3   *Actual profiles of secretarial activity at Figures*

N = 137

| Activity | Private secretary % of time | Secretary % of time | Typist % of time |
|---|---|---|---|
| Typing | 44 | 63.5 | 74.6 |
| Dictation | 11.7 | 6.8 | – |
| Mail | 6.5 | 4.6 | – |
| Filing | 4.2 | 1.0 | – |
| Errands | 2.0 | 1.0 | – |
| Admin. Assistant | 9.8 | 6.3 | – |
| Clerical | 8.8 | 4.2 | – |
| Personal time/other | 10.7 | 8.3 | 13.0 |
| Waiting for work | 2.3 | 4.3 | 12.4 |
| | 100.0 | 100.0 | 100.0 |

mail, filing, errands, administration and clerical tasks. It may be interesting to note from Table 2.3 that in terms of indices of inefficiency, in this case waiting for work, typists came out the worst (12.4 per cent of time), then came group secretaries (4.3 per cent of time) and then private secretaries (2.5 per cent of time). Again this situation can be readily explained. Typists are totally reliant on bosses for their work-load and its distribution. Group secretaries have some flexibility in terms of initiating activities on behalf of their bosses, thus it could be expected that they need not have much slack in their jobs; in fact it was only 4.3 per cent. Private secretaries have most responsibility and autonomy and in many cases strongly determine the design of their working day; this being the case, they would be expected to have little or no slack, and this has been empirically upheld in Figures, where the percentage was 2.3. Activities were not recorded before 9.00 a.m. or beyond 5.30 p.m. or during lunch hours; had they been, this statistic of 2.3 per cent would have been counterbalanced with a statistic indicating the amount of time spent in overtime. Overtime tends to be a hidden, but in some cases a significant, element of a private secretary's job. In addition, the very top six private secretaries were not included in this analysis, thus suppressing to some extent the actual profile of the private secretary in Figures.

## Secretaries' attitudes towards their jobs

The findings discussed in this section of the chapter are the results of the group discussions with all the secretarial staff.

### Recruitment and induction

On the whole, all the secretarial staff felt more strongly inclined towards talking about their job interviews than about their induction into Figures. Attitudes were not only more entrenched but also more negative towards the former than the latter. About half of the staff felt that they were not given a very accurate picture of the sort of work expected of them. This was particularly true for certain group secretaries and private secretaries. Although comments tended to be mixed, three main points emerged. Private secretaries were not told to expect so much copy typing, group secretaries were often informed that they would be working for less people than in fact was the situation, and private secretaries were not emphatically told that they would have to be prepared to help people other than their immediate bosses.

### Job content

In general, the secretarial staff were not enthusiastic about the over-all content of their jobs. This was particularly true for private secretaries and group secretaries. A characteristic of most of these secretaries was that they felt they were not applying their abilities to the full, and in so doing were being under-utilized by management. Most secretaries felt that copy typing accounted for the major proportion of their working day. A number of secretaries saw this as a task requiring low-level skills and one that could easily be undertaken by copy typists. Further, many of the secretaries, particularly those attached to groups of managers, referred to the 'tedious', 'monotonous' nature of copy typing. References were made to the frequent drafting and re-drafting of reports and accounts.

At a more general level, many of the private secretaries criticized the various definitions of a private secretary within Figures. While they appreciated that it was difficult for their bosses to delegate many tasks to them, owing to the technical nature of the work, they still felt capable of accepting more responsibility. More than a half of the private secretaries did not handle their bosses' telephone calls, while a smaller number neither dealt with their bosses' mail nor controlled their bosses' diaries. These three factors, coupled with the situation that most private secretaries were not physically located next door to their bosses, meant that private secretaries felt very detached from their managers. They sensed that their bosses were not interested in allowing them to be involved in their work. Some secretaries did not mind having this 'calculated working relationship', but the majority complained about it. 'It's a matter of using your initiative and doing what you're told here!' 'There are few avenues for initiative.' 'You're not expected to think. You're just expected to work like machines.'

Some of the secretaries felt that it was as much their responsibility as their bosses if they wanted a greater involvement in the bosses' work. Difficulties emerged, however, with a number of bosses who were apparently adamant that they should not delegate administrative tasks to their secretaries, despite the fact that they might be capable of carrying them out. This point was evidenced when bosses were absent from the office and secretaries acted as temporary surrogates — handling mail, telephone calls, and diaries. When this occurred the secretaries generally agreed that they were happy to assume these areas of responsibility and only wished that they were allowed to continue them when their bosses returned. Despite this recognition of the dual role played by private secretary and boss in expanding the former's job definition, the secretaries agreed that in the end it was the bosses' fault if they were not efficiently used. 'Bosses get the secretaries they deserve.' 'A secretary is only as good as her boss will let her be.'

Two private secretaries related this problem of under-utilization to the situation where the manager is allocated a private secretary for the first time. They felt that most bosses do not know how to use private secretaries.

In Figures there was an implicit assumption that all private secretaries should be willing to accept work from other members of management, providing they were not fully occupied by their own bosses. In general, private secretaries did not mind following this rule, but did not like doing work from different departments. This was for two reasons. First, they would be unfamiliar with the nature of the task, and were concerned about building up other departments' expectations of them. Secondly, they felt strongly that a degree of identification should be established for them in their working relationships.

## Work-load

In general, most secretarial staff thought they were kept reasonably busy in their jobs and that should a slack period occur, they could easily obtain alternative work. On a more critical note, a number of the group secretaries felt they were subjected to too much pressure. Specifically, a number of problems were highlighted by them.

Work-loads among the secretaries were uneven. Although it was not possible to equate one manager's work-load with another's, some secretaries felt that they provided a service for a far greater number of managers than others, and that in some cases their bosses could be located in three different departments. This was problematic when the secretary was faced with 'urgent' work from several bosses simultaneously. According to the secretaries, priorities on work in such situations could more easily be established if all the items requiring their attention derived from the same department.

Secretaries and typists did not mind working overtime in cases where urgent work was genuinely needed. In fact, many of the secretaries said that they frequently worked during the lunch hour and/or stayed late in the evening. One referred to 'black Fridays', since this was the day she was most likely to be requested to stay on. She, like the majority of secretaries and typists, did not resent doing overtime for her boss if her effort was acknowledged and appreciated. However, many of the secretaries said that work which was frequently described as 'urgent' was not in fact needed for several days. In such circumstances, they felt unnecessarily pressurized.

On the whole, secretaries helped one another in order to control the work-load. Most private secretaries said that they were prepared to work for managers other than their bosses, although references were made to certain 'prima donnas' among them who would not conform to this arrangement. This could be partly explained by the fact that a number of private secretaries said they were not specifically told to expect this at their job interviews. There was a danger that where private secretaries did accept work from managers other than their immediate bosses, an over-all 'creeping commitment' could emerge, whereby it became embarrassing to refuse to help, even when they were fully occupied with work from their own bosses.

## Attitude of boss(es)

Attitudes towards how the secretarial staff were treated by their bosses were generally very favourable. This was particularly true for private secretaries across all departments, who revealed strong work commitments to their bosses. This was significant in terms of the importance placed on this aspect of secretarial work. The only group who objected to the attitudes of their bosses was one of the typist pools. They felt that their efforts were rarely acknowledged. In sum, they appeared to experience strong feelings of alienation within their department: 'We're just treated as inferior beings.' 'We're not thought of as individuals.'

While the general impression towards bosses was a favourable one, a number of minor criticisms were made. Some of the managers were identified as being somewhat inconsiderate and, on occasions, even rude. Examples were quoted of how work was just left on the secretary's desk, with no note of explanation attached to it, so that she did not even know who had left it. Items of work were given to secretaries/typists with no 'please' or 'thank you', and this was particularly upsetting when the secretary had stayed late in order to complete the work. In relation to the last point, several secretaries described experiences of staying late in order to complete 'urgent' work, which was then not collected for two to three days afterwards.

A particular bone of contention was the company's typing layout. A minority of secretaries and managers did not adhere to the manual. The secretaries who did strictly follow the manual resented others who did not do likewise. In some cases specific clients or members of management did not want documents typed according to the company layout. In such circumstances, the secretaries/typists needed to be briefed on this. One secretary said that she had been obliged to re-type completely a set of documents because of a lack of briefing on layout.

Another aspect of this lack of information clarity was also raised. Secretaries complained that they often did not know where their bosses were because they so frequently left their offices without informing them. This could cause embarrassment and unnecessary difficulties to secretaries when asked for the location of their bosses.

It was suggested that better presentation of drafts to secretaries and typists would save a lot of typing time. Bad writing was frequently identified as a primary factor leading to inefficiency. If management took more care over their drafts, clarified technical words, and spent some time instructing the typist on the nature of the work, then this situation would be greatly improved. Further, when re-drafts were submitted, amendments should be clearly inserted in the appropriate places.

In addition to the above comments on the submission of drafts, all the secretarial staff agreed that if letters were approved before being typed and if there was greater co-ordination by management in over-seeing reports and accounts, then perhaps a number of the draft stages could be eliminated. This would probably constitute a major saving in typing time.

A number of management were criticized for being inefficient at giving dictation. One secretary mentioned that two hours of dictation might culminate in one hour of typing. Another said that when she was called into her boss's office for dictation, she was usually expected to stay there, even if the boss was interrupted by telephone calls. The latter could last up to one hour. This was an extremely time wasting use of secretaries: 'Bosses don't think about what secretaries have to do.'

Several secretaries objected to the way their bosses checked up on the tasks they carried out; they sensed that their bosses did not place much confidence in them. Allied to this issue were strong complaints from the secretaries at one location that their arrival and departure times were carefully watched. They said that according to this system no recognition was given to them for coming in early, working lunch hours, or staying late. At the same time, they felt that they were being 'earmarked' by management if they came in five minutes late or left five minutes early. 'They don't have any faith in their secretaries.'

While secretaries generally wanted the opportunity for greater responsibility in their jobs, conversely they also wished that their bosses would try to develop a greater understanding of the demands of the secretary's job. Several examples were given of where they had been asked to complete work within impossible deadlines, or where they were perceived to have 'nothing to do' if their bosses were out of the office. One private secretary said that she had the impression that if her boss had no impending work on his desk, he immediately assumed that his private secretary had nothing to do. 'Once it's (work) off his desk, he thinks it's done!'

### Salary

Over-all reactions to salary were favourable. Most of the secretarial staff felt that they compared quite well with the average rates for London. While a number mentioned that they could probably get higher salaries elsewhere, they added that they were 'very happy' in their jobs and that was the most important thing to them.

In general, secretaries seemed to be fairly ignorant of others' salaries and of pay scales in general. A few criticized the way in which they had seen others negotiate salaries on joining the company. Some mentioned that they felt there were not large enough differentials between ages and grades. There were mixed feelings towards the six-monthly salary reviews. The majority of secretaries perceived the December rise to be based on the cost of living, and the June rise to be based on merit, but there was a lot of confusion surrounding this. It was apparent that a number of secretaries did not realize that there was a merit rise system. Among those who did know of it, reactions varied. Some saw it as a 'good system', while others felt that it didn't really differentiate between the high and low performers. In addition, several mentioned that the June merit rise could cause some resentment in the office, since those not getting an increase could see others receiving 'the white envelopes' which enclosed information on their salary rises.

## Career appraisal and development within the company

Most secretaries seemed to have a good idea of how they were progressing in their jobs. Comments from one department were, however, particularly negative, since a number of the secretarial staff there neither saw their performance appraisals nor discussed their work with their bosses.

Perceptions of performance appraisal forms from the secretarial staff of other departments varied: 'They act to encourage you.' 'They raise false hopes.' 'They don't make an iota of difference.'

Some secretaries complained that annual staff meetings were often cancelled, or if they did take place, that they were very superficial and showed little interest in the secretaries. In contrast, other secretarial staff spoke highly of their experiences of annual staff meetings.

With regard to wanting the opportunity to move to another department, most of the secretaries agreed that they were happy to stay where they were. However, a number of them said that they wished secretarial appointments were advertised internally, as was the policy for management appointments. They felt that they were being rather 'ignored' because of this: 'Girls have as much right to careers here as men.' 'It isn't company policy to transfer staff [secretarial] internally.'

In general, the majority of secretaries did not see the prospect of becoming a private secretary as very attractive. They felt that although such a promotion did bring with it more administrative tasks and less typing, on the whole they did not regard it as a 'noticeable step up' their career ladders. They indicated that if they really wanted to advance their secretarial careers, they would have to look at opportunities outside Figures.

★ ★ ★

The main focus of this case study has been in looking at the secretarial role in a particular organizational context from the secretaries' point of view rather than from their bosses' perspective. It is valuable in terms of alerting management, the personnel function, and organizations in general, to a number of general problems surrounding secretaries. These may be broadly summarized under eight headings.

## 1 Dependence on temporary secretarial staff

To what extent is your company using temporary staff? Why does your company use temporary staff at all? This last question should be answered by analysing the kind of secretarial demands your company has; for example, does the work consist primarily of routine copy typing? If the work requires several days induction or training in the company's systems then it may not be appropriate to use temporary staff on a weekly basis. It will take up too much of managers/other secretaries/personnel time to train the temporary secretaries, and no sooner are they trained than they will probably be leaving. Another factor to be considered here is to what extent work is allocated to secretaries in your company on an informal basis. In other words, if secretaries have to be well integrated socially into the company before they are efficiently used, then this militates against employing temporary staff. A last general caveat to using temporary secretaries is that they can cause unrest and resentment among the permanent staff if they continually complain about the unattractiveness of the company as a place to work. Temporary secretarial staff are more easily able to do this since they are uncommitted to the company. This is, however, only likely to occur in situations where the permanent secretaries are already feeling dissatisfied with their jobs.

## 2 Inaccurate job expectations

How does your company handle secretarial recruitment and selection? It is vitally important that potential candidates for secretarial posts are given information which is as accurate as possible — and this applies from the advertisement, to the briefing by the agency (if used), to the initial interview with personnel, through to the final interview with the boss. A vulnerable link in this process tends to be the interview with the boss. It is extremely important that he prepares for this interview situation in order that an accurate profile is given of the job and conversely that the relevant information concerning the job applicant is obtained. The cost of not carrying out this process efficiently is not only in terms of the inconvenience and unhappiness to the boss and secretary, but also in terms of the ever increasing financial investment involved in recruiting another secretary.

### 3  The job content of the secretarial job

In so many situations secretaries are vastly over-qualified for the jobs they are doing. This point links up with the previous one of recruitment and selection of secretarial staff. If the job really is a copy typing job then do not employ a highly skilled secretary for it, because she will be wasting her talents and will probably be frustrated in the process. How many organizations know how they are using their secretarial staff, and more importantly, how many organizations understand how they *should* be using their secretarial staff? So many management training courses attempt to teach managers all the up-to-date techniques available to them in their jobs, yet omit to teach them how to use their most critical resource: their private secretary. Individual bosses should take the time to sit down with their secretaries and work out jointly how many tasks could effectively be delegated to the latter. It seems ridiculous that while so many managers are complaining about being over-pressurized in their jobs, so many of the same managers' secretaries are complaining about being under-utilized!

### 4  Planning work-loads

It often seems as though bosses and secretaries do not realize that they should be working together as teams. Just as it is critical for the manager to plan ahead, so this is also true of his secretary. Of course, unpredictable events do occur which mean that the secretary may suddenly be faced with work, but on the whole, many of the secretarial panics are due to bosses not planning and liaising their work adequately with their secretaries. Allied to this point of planning work-loads with the secretary, is the issue of establishing priorities. It is essential to set priorities on work when giving it to a secretary. If the boss-secretary relationship is being managed effectively, then usually she will already know what these priorities are. If the boss is in any doubt, however, it is wise to ensure that these priorities are made quite explicit to the secretary. In setting priorities with the secretary, be realistic. If the work really is required by the end of the afternoon, then the secretary may have to stay a little late in order to complete it. If, however, the work is not required for two days, it is extremely annoying for the secretary to be told that it is wanted urgently. This is a blatant abuse of the secretary and such abuse normally leads to the boss losing her respect. This next point is only a matter of common courtesy, but it is nice if managers show their gratitude to their secretarial staff when they do put themselves out to get work completed for them.

### 5   Giving work to secretaries

A major saving in secretarial costs can be made by bosses taking a little time in ensuring that drafts are in good order, and by properly briefing secretaries on the work. It is no good after the event telling the secretary that you meant the report to be typed with double spacing. Again, where a manager has his own secretary, then briefing should not be a major problem. If a report or document has to be agreed by a number of managers, it is also inefficient to get it re-typed each time any one individual makes suggestions for modifications. This can be a very time wasting and tedious procedure for the secretary. If a lot of the organization's work does consist of reports which go through several stages of re-writing, then it is ideally suited to using word processing units. Briefing secretaries is extremely important. One important point which should always be made clear to the secretary is whether the document is in its draft or final stage; a lot of time can be wasted in producing an immaculate document only to learn that it is only a first draft.

### 6   Involvement in the work

If all the above points are applied to the management of the boss-secretary relationship, then it follows that the secretary should feel a personal identification and involvement in the manager's work. Such personal involvement can be developed by having regular discussions with the secretary. During these talks problems experienced by either the manager or secretary can be identified and analysed; and suggestions can be made for improving current systems and procedures in the office. In general, the objective of these discussions/meetings should be to show a genuine interest in sharing one another's work. A secretary and boss can only work together harmoniously if there is a meaningful understanding of each other's role. An important repercussion of having such a boss-secretary relationship is that the secretary should be able to take the initiative in her work activities. She understands her boss's job so she should be able to anticipate his needs. A secretary should never be in a position of being bored and waiting for work; she should always know how to use her time effectively.

### 7   Career development

Bosses, and at a more general level, organizations, should show an interest in and participate in the planning of their secretaries' careers. If the boss-secretary relationship is managed in the close, supportive way that is being advocated in this book, then the secretary should automatically be receiving regular feedback on her performance. On a more formal basis there should be a proper performance appraisal each year. This should be carried out in the context of the secretary's job description, which should emanate from point 3 above (that is, the discussion and agreement on the secretary's job content). During the performance appraisal both secretary and boss should have the opportunity to propose ways in which the secretary could develop in her job. This may include the need for further training. On a different level, personnel should publicize secretarial vacancies, thus informing the secretarial staff of the job opportunities available to them. This process, in fact, should not stop at secretarial vacancies. Some secretaries may be able and keen to move into a different kind of position, for example, into personnel or line management, and such opportunities should not be closed off to secretaries. Unfortunately, secretaries are frequently stereotyped in a narrow, over restrictive way in terms of their progression in organizations. Many secretaries, however, have had substantial experience relevant to a position in management. It is a great shame that organizations traditionally dismiss this large pool of potential talent when putting together their management structure.

## 8 *Management of the secretarial function*
It is impossible to recommend one effective way of managing the secretarial function in all types of organizations. The issue should be carefully analysed, however, in the light of such factors as number of secretarial staff, and dispersion across functions, departments, and physical locations. There are advantages in centralizing the responsibility of all secretarial staff to one person in the company. In this way, the person has a complete overview of the total secretarial staff, and all secretarial staff are treated in a uniform way. It is this person's responsibility to make sure that secretarial jobs are properly defined and that secretaries are used efficiently. Unfortunately, where this job position does exist in companies, it is usually defined at a fairly low level, thus restricting control in a key area. The person filling this post should be very carefully selected; it has to be someone who can hold his/her own *vis-à-vis* the rest of the management team, and at the same time identify closely with the secretarial staff.

In some companies the complete operational and administrative responsibilities of the secretarial staff are split. (Of course, where private secretaries are concerned, the operational responsibilities reside with their parallel bosses.) The top private secretary in a section may be responsible for all the secretarial work carried out in her department. She is therefore the person in charge of allocation of secretarial work and quality control. This can be an attractive system since it develops a departmental cohesiveness among all the secretarial staff (this is particularly important at the lower levels), as well as creating some job enrichment for the top secretaries in terms of having staff responsibilities. In my experience this arrangement usually encourages a good supportive relationship between secretaries working in the same deparfment. This kind of system capitalizes on the existing informal relationships that have usually developed between such secretaries.

## Conclusion

In conclusion, if this case study illustrates only one point, it is that secretaries are all too often regarded by management as items of expenditure on the payroll rather than as individuals who are seeking challenge and self-fulfilment in their jobs. Not enough care is given in organizations to finding out what really motivates secretaries, and this is a great paradox because what most motivates them probably involves managers using them most effectively. It is no surprise that in a large organizational study of secretaries in the United States it was discovered that secretaries at all levels in the organization strongly valued and desired personal feelings of accomplishment and growth in their jobs. The more secretaries perceived their jobs to be motivating, the more satisfied they were with their jobs. Further, this relationship was linked to position in the secretarial hierarchy; that is, the higher the secretary was in the organization, the more she tended to have a motivating job and, in consequence, derived greater job satisfaction. The problem is that many secretaries are not willing to wait patiently until they reach the top of the organization before achieving job satisfaction. Further, the ones who drop out lower down are sometimes the best performers who simply cannot tolerate their job frustration any longer.

# 3 The Varying Roles of Private Secretaries

In Chapter 1 I characterized movement up the secretarial hierarchy in terms of the changing dependency relationship between boss and secretary. At the bottom of the hierarchy the secretary (or more precisely, the pool typist) is clearly dependent on her boss(es) for her work activities. The latter consists almost entirely of typing, hence the typist has a mechanistic role. (It is interesting to note here that when typewriters were originally introduced into this country, their operators were also known as 'typewriters'. Thus the human being in this work process was depersonalized and merged with the identity of the machine.) At the top of the organization this dependency relationship shifts such that the boss depends heavily upon his private secretary. Her role is more organic in nature, consisting of a large proportion of self-initiating administrative tasks rather than routine typing. The differing nature of the secretarial role throughout the hierarchy was illustrated in the case study described in the last chapter.

It is the discretionary element inherent in top private secretaries' jobs which most interested me. In a desire to develop a greater understanding of how such secretaries define their work roles, I carried out five in-depth interviews. The secretaries were located in two contrasting organizations: an educational establishment, and a large manufacturing company. All five secretaries held very different types of organizational positions. They were selected for interview on account of this fact. During the interviews no attempt was made at asking an identical set of questions. Instead, the questions were stimulated by the comments made by each of the secretaries during the course of the interview. This chapter begins by describing the outcome of those five interviews, in terms of how each secretary saw her work role. At the end of the chapter I have tried to identify and discuss the most salient factors which seemed to determine the roles these secretaries played. A general framework is then presented which summarizes the factors determining the nature of the secretarial role, and how the secretarial role can be defined.

*Sheila, private secretary to the head of a university department*
Sheila, aged 37, had held her particular secretarial job for eight and a half years; she joined the university following several years of experience with a number of commercial organizations. The department was large, consisting of about 100 staff and about 300 full-time students. Sheila's decision to be a secretary was, she felt, less of a conscious career choice than of merely accepting what was at that time regarded to be a traditional occupation for girls. She thought that if she was today at the school leaving age, she would not have hesitated in continuing her education at university.

When Sheila first started as a secretary at the university, she had her own part-time assistant, who undertook the filing and some of the typing. When she left, however, Sheila found it impossible to obtain a replacement, and so the assistant position had now disappeared. Sheila was able to cope in the absence of any help owing to a reduction in the number of meetings she was asked to attend in the course of her job. While she had to go to a considerable number in the 'early days', she now had to attend only two each year. The administrative officer or her boss took the minutes at all other internal meetings in which her boss participated. In general, Sheila very rarely left her office during the course of the working day. She attended very few meetings, and never accompanied her boss on outside visits. This aspect of the job fitted in closely with Sheila's own perception of the private secretarial position. She felt that one of the primary role demands of the private secretary was constant accessibility in her office. She considered this function to be particularly important if a boss spent considerable periods away from the office. For this reason, Sheila kept regular hours — 9.00 a.m.-5.15 p.m. — although in the summer when her boss was less busy, she came in an hour later. She was rarely required to do 'overtime'; when this did occur it was because of impending circumstances and usually necessitated her staying an extra hour at the office. She never worked at week-ends. Contrary to the practices of certain bosses at the university, Sheila's boss never contacted her at home out of office hours.

When her boss was absent, Sheila felt she was not able to take over many of his tasks, for example, responding to letters on behalf of him. The latter she usually delegated to one of her boss's subordinates, or she would write a letter of acknowledgement informing the recipient that her boss would deal with the issue on his return. The reason for this was that most of the requests for information from her boss took the form of asking for his personal opinion on a variety of issues; obviously, Sheila was unable to reply to these herself. In contrast, Sheila said that in her last job as private secretary to a sales manager, she was able to reply on his behalf to a number of letters, since many of these were customer queries. In this situation Sheila recognized that her boss had evolved a fairly standard set of rules/procedures for dealing with such correspondence. As such, she had found it easy to learn how to reply to customer queries. Sheila felt that there was less of a 'programmed' element to her current boss's job in terms of processing incoming information. Since her current boss was head of a large department, the kinds of decisions he made were usually allied to planning and policy-making. They tended, therefore, to be complex, one-off decisions. On account of her boss's job, Sheila did not see her position as offering many opportunities for initiating activities. In general, she relied to a great extent upon her boss's explicit instructions in carrying out her work, and this was no problem since he came into the office most days. In fact, Sheila's day usually began by a meeting with him to discuss and plan the day's activities. She estimated that she spent at least a total of forty minutes a day with her boss in this way. This meant that Sheila was continually in close touch with him. In addition, since he never went away on business for long blocks of time, she was never required to manage the office in his total absence. Sheila suggested that an important characteristic of her (and her boss's) work was its relatively slow pace. Deadlines were virtually non-existent, so this meant that there were few secretarial panics at the office. This slow pace, together with her regular access to her boss, led Sheila to describe her position as 'not very demanding'. Certainly in terms of analysing her time, Sheila's job did appear to consist of many low-level activities. Typing took up a lot of her time, closely followed by photocopying. The most interesting aspect of her activity profile, though, was that the largest proportion of her day was spent in dealing with the constant personal interruptions.

These interruptions came from every level in the department: from the most junior lecturer to a senior professor. Although there was a recognized hierarchy in the department — students, lecturers, senior lecturers, professors, and deputy head — anyone could go and speak to the head of department. The department encouraged openness and informality. The natural repercussion of this practice was that Sheila spent a lot of time dealing with personal interruptions, which either ended up with her arranging quick meetings with her boss, or just acquiring the information from him herself.

In many respects Sheila enjoyed the wide-ranging contacts she maintained in the department. She was not isolated like many other comparable top secretaries she knew of in other companies. Secondly, she was able to keep in touch with current issues of debate throughout the department, which meant she was able to keep her boss informed as to what was going on. This allowed him to be closer to his staff and students in a way that would usually be denied to him. Sheila rather prided herself with respect to this; she knew she was an important source of information to him. A third repercussion of the informal communication system in the department, was that Sheila and all the other secretaries arranged most of their bosses' meetings during coffee and tea breaks. This was easy because all staff and students congregated in one large communal area for coffee and tea. Sheila's heavy reliance on personal contacts within the department distinguished the top secretarial job which she had. She concluded by saying that while her position was by no means intellectually demanding, this was more than compensated for by the friendly personal approach she was able to bring to her job.

### Janet, private secretary to the chairman of Heavy Metal

Janet, who was in her late thirties, had worked for the chairman for nineteen years, thus representing her total experience of private secretarial work. Sir Ernest Matthews (Sir M. as he was known) became chairman of the company in 1973 following the death of his predecessor. Janet quickly pointed out to me that much of her work derived not from her boss's position in the Heavy Metal Company as such, but from the numerous other organizations in which he was active. He was, for instance, Chairman of the Industrial Council, a member of two government boards, as well as being a governor to a number of schools throughout the country. Janet was not 'officially' obliged to assist Sir M. on any work derivative from his participation in these outside organizations, but as yet she had never refused him her assistance.

Janet's office was immediately adjacent to her boss's; its situation being such that any person wanting to speak to Sir M. would have to go via her office. Since there was only a small number of personnel at headquarters, Janet said that she did not experience any problems in terms of having to screen anyone from seeing her boss. Although Sir M. was very busy, Janet said that he was always ready to see the deputy chairman, or any other director should the latter ever call into Janet's office informally. Such *ad hoc* meetings tended not to last longer than five to ten minutes.

Sir M. came into his office most days. Some hours, though, would be spent at meetings held either at his office or other company locations in Great Britain. On account of this, Sir M. had a personal chauffeur. Janet was never requested to be present at any of these functions: where the latter consisted of meetings with the directors, the company secretary usually took the minutes. Sir M.'s visits overseas tended not to constitute more than three to four weeks in the year (either taken in one block, or broken into one-week units), during which time he would go to the branches of Heavy Metal in Canada, South Africa, and Australia. On such occasions Janet usually remained at the office, although once she went to South Africa for a week. The purpose of this trip was to clear an exceptional backlog of work which had accumulated at the London office during her boss's absence.

Until one month previous to our interview, Janet had undertaken the full range of secretarial tasks for her boss. This had meant that in the past she had been kept constantly busy, since he regularly had a considerable amount of outgoing correspondence to be typed, together with a heavy quantity of incoming mail which had to be processed. She told me that the work-load so pressurized her that she rarely went home before 6.30 p.m. each day, and even then she found it difficult to find time for filing. While working at such a pace Janet found that she never had more time than just to glance at the incoming mail. Sir M. had decided recently, however, that he wanted her to participate more in the handling of the incoming mail, since he felt that his own time was becoming increasingly restricted. He told Janet that he felt her primary role should be 'to reduce the paperwork to him as much as possible'. Consequently, Janet has become an 'interpreter of information' for her boss. A second secretary had been employed (Kerry) and she undertook all the shorthand and typing for him. Although Janet continued to receive and make telephone calls for her boss, this was to be altered soon so that the second secretary would handle them completely. In addition, Kerry was learning the filing, and Janet hoped that when she had familiarized herself with the system, she would be able to take over most of this task.

During the day most of Janet's time was taken up in scanning the incoming mail to her boss. Certain pieces, like invitations to take out subscriptions to magazines and information on forthcoming seminars and conferences, she usually threw away, since she felt that her boss's time was already heavily committed to other activities. There were three seminars run each year by the British Institute of Management which she knew did interest him, from his past participation in them, and thus any information arising about them was automatically kept. When Janet felt that the magazine/seminar might be of interest to another person in Heavy Metal, she would re-route the relevant information to that person. Janet, however, tended not to discard invitations to seminars for Sir M. where these were personally addressed to him, even though she felt that the subject-matter might not interest him sufficiently to want to attend. Other letters that Janet immediately redirected internally included correspondence from people seeking jobs in Heavy Metal, irrespective of the individual's background.

Most of Janet's reading time was spent in studying the incoming magazines, publications, minutes from various meetings, reports, etc. In each case she read the document as thoroughly as possible, and then drew her boss's attention to what she regarded as being the most important points mentioned. She did this by drawing red lines beside the appropriate sentences. When this procedure was completed, the document was then forwarded to her boss.

Where a letter/memo requested an appointment with Sir M., Janet automatically arranged a date. The date was then regarded as 'firm' unless cancelled by him later. (This control over a boss's diary is a feature that is not characteristic of all private secretarial positions.) In some cases outsiders who were not personally acquainted with Sir M. telephoned in order to arrange appointments with him. When this occurred and Janet was in doubt as to whether her boss would like to see the person concerned, she asked the caller to write an official letter requesting such a meeting. On receipt of the letter, she would then either forward it directly to her boss or pass it on to another director. Where a letter required a reply from her boss, Janet would pass it on to Sir M., together with any necessary background files.

Two other tasks Janet performed were arranging travel and lunches for her boss. The company did not channel all its travel business through an agency, and consequently control over this lay with the individual private secretary. There was an administrative officer at the head office who, among other duties, was in charge of dining arrangements, and thus Janet negotiated all her boss's luncheon dates through her. Once every week/fortnight Janet prepared a diary of her boss's activities; this was typed and copies circulated to him, the deputy chairman, the chairman's wife, his personal driver, and Kerry, while retaining a copy for her own use.

Outside of these main activities, Janet was ready to assist her boss at any time on any task that might evolve in the course of the day. While I was there she was asked to help him in the preparation of the 200 long-service certificates that would be awarded at the forthcoming annual company dinner.

On the whole Janet's working day did not alter much from one day to the next in terms of the hours she spent at the office. She always arrived at 9.00 a.m. and left at around 6.00-6.30 p.m., taking 1.00-2.00 p.m. for her lunch hour. She said that she had never been asked specifically to work overtime (the official hours were 9.00-5.00), but did so in order to prevent work from accumulating. She felt, however, that the tendency for the latter to arise would be greatly diminished since Kerry had joined the company.

### Kerry, second private secretary to the chairman of Heavy Metal

Kerry was, in contrast to Janet, much younger (in her mid-twenties) and thus had far less secretarial experience, albeit that it was gained from working in a number of different companies. Kerry had been working for Heavy Metal for four weeks.

Kerry was very pessimistic about the restructuring of the private secretary role to the chairman. She doubted the effectiveness of dividing Janet's original set of activities between the two of them. Not only did she question the efficiency of the system on the basis of costs, but also on the level of job satisfaction of Janet and herself. During this period of adjustment to Heavy Metal, Kerry was only handling most of the chairman's outgoing mail, i.e. she was responsible for all the shorthand and typing that he required. Once she had learned the filing system, she would also help Janet with that task. After only one week at Heavy Metal, Kerry complained to the chairman about the lack of involvement she experienced, and of her intention to resign from her post. In an attempt to meet the problem he had arranged for Kerry to handle all the telephone calls for him. This was being carried out. Kerry, however, did not regard this as a solution to her problem. Kerry's office was located around the corner to Janet's; this meant that every time a query was raised on the phone she had to 'buzz' Janet, who might in turn have to consult Sir M. This would certainly occur where the query was linked to past correspondence which was filed in Janet's office. (Kerry kept no files in her office.) In view of this, Kerry thought she would merely serve as another intermediary link between the chairman and his contacts, extending the already complicated communication chain.

Kerry felt that all the aspects of a private secretarial job were so interrelated that it was impossible to divide the tasks 'neatly' between two private secretaries. The only way she envisaged Janet being able to relieve her work-load was if she had a shorthand typist who functioned as *her* personal assistant. In this way Janet retained complete control over all the work; she merely delegated to the assistant when she was overburdened. In sum, Kerry felt she was an 'appendix' to the chairman and Janet, and as such felt very alienated in her position.

### Christine, private secretary to the group marketing director of Heavy Metal

Christine was in her early forties, married, and had a family. She had had considerable experience in secretarial work (fifteen years), during which time she had worked in four different companies. She joined Heavy Metal in 1972 when she was appointed as private secretary to the group marketing director. Two months previous to this interview her boss had been made chairman of Heavy Buildings, a subsidiary company within the Building Division of Heavy Metal. This had meant that he now had to spend extended periods of time at the company's base in Birmingham as well as making regular visits abroad. At the time of being interviewed, Christine's boss was in Germany attending a conference. Since his appointment as chairman of Heavy Buildings he was spending on average three days per fortnight at the London offices. This had led to important changes in Christine's work pattern. Basically it meant that she did not have a regular work routine; instead, she distinguished two types: one associated with the days her boss came into the office, and the other connected with the time her boss was absent from it. When the former occurred, Christine's hours were usually 8.30 a.m.-6.00 p.m., and when the latter occurred they were 9.30 a.m.-4.00 p.m. (Christine mentioned that one of the privileges of a good secretarial job was the ability of the individual to fix her own working hours.)

When her boss, Mr Heart, came into the office most of Christine's day was spent in handling correspondence. Christine regarded her boss as very efficient and systematic. Since he liked to deal with matters as promptly as possible, Christine felt she had to reciprocate by typing all his letters the same day that he had given them to her, even if this meant staying later than 6.00 p.m. Initially Christine sorted the morning's incoming mail and took it into her boss together with the letters and other memos and messages which had arrived over the past fortnight. The latter was classified into two files, the one which Christine regarded as requiring urgent action, and the other which required reading when her boss had attended to more pressing business. Examples of the contents of such files were suggested to me. In the file for 'urgent action' Christine would place any letters needing a quick decision, in most cases these pertained to policy issues inside the Heavy Metal group. In the file containing information of less importance, Christine would put minutes from past executive and board meetings, together with agendas for such forthcoming meetings. When an agenda contained an issue which was to be raised/commented on by her boss, Christine would draw his attention to it. She might even put such a document in the file for 'urgent action' if she felt that he would have to spend some time working on the issue at hand. In general, then, Christine allocated priorities to information on the basis of whether her boss needed to take action on it or not. If action was required, the relevant document got a high priority. Among all documents requiring action, priorities were then placed in terms of how soon steps needed to be taken.

Apart from dealing with mail, Christine also gave an informal report to her boss of telephone messages she had received for him, and issues which she had handled or delegated to someone else during his absence. Christine emphasized that looking after her boss's diary was one of the most important tasks in her job. Although she had the authority to make appointments for him, his secretary in Birmingham (she was a private secretary to one of his colleagues, but he had access to her) was also likely to make some dates for him, and on occasions Mr Heart would make his own private arrangements. Thus Mr Heart had a pocket diary and desk diary, while both Christine and Mr Heart's secretary in Birmingham had duplicate desk diaries. When the secretary in Birmingham typed the occasional letter or arranged a meeting for Mr Heart, such tasks would be co-ordinated with Christine. It was the latter's responsibility, then, to centralize all her boss's meetings for him. This she did mainly through regular contact with the secretary in Birmingham, the secretaries at head office and Mr Heart; if he was abroad she would write and inform him of the meetings she had planned for him. Christine attached the utmost importance to the planning of her boss's diary, as Mr Heart was constantly being invited to meetings and conferences. The problem was to try and integrate all his commitments.

On the days when Mr Heart did not come into head office, Christine's work pace slackened considerably. Initially, she sorted any incoming mail, as usual. She would deal with some of it herself where this was possible; this would consist of internal letters requesting certain information from Mr Heart, which Christine could easily locate herself. It might also include requests for meetings, invitations to seminars, queries about certain issues in which Mr Heart was involved. In the situation where Christine was unable to deal with the issue and knew her boss would not be in for at least another four days, she would send an acknowledgement informing the recipient that her boss would deal with the matter on his return. This procedure might be unnecessary if Christine felt that the issue could easily be delegated to another manager, as had occurred in a number of cases. The decision to delegate, and to whom the document should be delegated to, was related closely to Christine's perceptions of Mr Heart's own practices. In exceptional circumstances Christine would forward particular correspondence to her boss, this then allowed him the option of dealing with it immediately. Where this occurred, he might telephone a draft letter to her, which would be transcribed, typed, and sent off by Christine to the person concerned.

Christine said that, on average, 90 per cent of the information she handled for her boss was allied to intra-organizational issues (i.e. within the Heavy Metal group), and only 10 per cent derived from the outside environment. Such a ratio, she suggested, might be very different for the private secretary to the sales director, where she hypothesized that 70 per cent of information might come from inter-organizational contacts and only 30 per cent from intra-organizational ones. Since most of the information Christine handled came from within Heavy Metal, she did not receive many telephone calls for Mr Heart in his absence, as most of his peers and subordinates knew of his movements. When she received a phone call for Mr Heart and he was not in the office, she would initially try to deal with it herself. Failing this, she would assess the importance of the matter and as a result might give the caller her boss's telephone number abroad, or his number at home, whichever was the most convenient.

Since Christine's boss was absent from the office so much, she could be seen to operate not only as an 'interpreter of information' for him, but also as an important 'allocator of her boss's time'. The latter may be evaluated as a higher order role, since Christine was able to function as an 'allocator of her boss's time' only after she had completed the initial stage of 'interpreting the information input', allied to the request for her boss's time. In this allocation role, Christine could be seen to undertake two principal tasks:

1 She decided which incoming information should be filtered through to her boss, in terms of both written and verbal information.

2 With respect to the information she could direct to her boss, she allocated a certain priority/delay factor, e.g. she classified the incoming mail into that which required immediate attention and that which could be delayed. She also decided when to arrange

meetings. If meetings 'clashed', she made a decision as to which should have priority; she also determined the duration of meetings, in terms of compiling a programme of commitments for her boss.

Christine's boss depended upon her for the carrying out of these duties, but such tasks necessitated value judgements to be made by Christine. Therefore it was possible that where Christine's value judgements deviated significantly from her boss's, the result could be perceived to be somewhat dysfunctional to him.

It was for this reason that Christine felt that it was essential for a private secretary to be 'involved in her job'. She must familiarize herself with all aspects of her boss's job, and this included reading in detail all his incoming mail, and being aware of how he handled all matters emerging in the course of his work. In this way the private secretary gradually 'learns' her boss's responses to the various situations he is exposed to in the course of his job, and as a result, the private secretary is able to function as a surrogate in his absence.

Private secretaries' job situations vary considerably in terms of their bosses' frequency of absence from the office. As a general statement, however, Christine posited that the frequency tended to increase 'up the organization'. The only exception she offered to this was the sales department; any manager working in this section would probably be absent often, although again this frequency might increase in ascending the organization.

Christine felt that certain problems did ensue for the private secretary whose boss was absent a lot. In her particular job situation where Mr Heart was away for, on average, seven working days out of every ten, she found that she was increasingly becoming very frustrated. Since there was rarely any typing left to be done in his absence, Christine found that she had extended periods of complete inactivity between deliveries of the mail, punctuated only by the occasional telephone call. Christine told me that she regarded the essential ingredient of a satisfying private secretarial job to be variety of tasks, a feeling of involvement, and being kept busy. Since the latter aspect had recently been lacking in her job she had asked her boss whether she might take on extra work from other secretaries at the office. As Mr Heart was extremely reluctant for this to happen, Christine was considering leaving the company, unless it was possible for her to be transferred to another part of Heavy Metal. Christine seemed to resent her boss's wish for her to work exclusively for him as his work did not occupy all her time. She stated that this manifestation of 'total possession of the private secretary' was shown often by managers; she thought that bosses regarded their private secretaries as status symbols and that this was one of the reasons why they were reluctant to share them with their peers. A second reason was that a secretary's inactivity might be regarded as a reflection of her boss's inactivity.

Over all, Christine distinguished bosses in terms of four characteristics. First, bosses varied in terms of the extent to which they expected their secretaries to carry out on their behalf personally oriented tasks — for example, shopping. Christine said that she felt abused by her boss when used in this way. When this had occurred with a previous employer, she did not have the courage to confront him about the incident, but she had felt a great deal of resentment about it. The second way in which bosses differ was in the manner in which they organized their work. Some liked to work regular office hours, while others preferred to arrive late and leave late, and expect the private secretary to do likewise. One boss Christine knew of never bothered reading the post until the afternoon and this invariably meant that the private secretary would be expected to stay on to type out replies to the letters. Christine thought it was important for a private secretary to be able to adapt to her boss's routine; if she felt she could not accept it and could not 'convert' him, then it was probably best to leave. It was essential, Christine said, for a private secretary to be able to work 'with her boss', to believe in both what he/she does, and how it is carried out. Christine said she could not work for someone whose decisions she did not respect.

A third way in which bosses differed, Christine believed, was the degree to which they delegated tasks to their secretaries. Some allowed their private secretaries very little discretion; for instance, they never let them arrange appointments for them without consultation first, or let them draft letters on their behalf. Allied to this aspect of delegation is the autonomy allowed to the private secretary in carrying out her work. Christine told me that when she was transcribing a draft from her boss, she was able to make modifications to it if she thought it was necessary, but this was something that not all bosses were liable to approve. Some bosses, she said, tended not to allow their secretaries to use any initiative in their jobs. However, as Christine pointed out, this was difficult where the private secretary worked for a busy director at the top of a company, who was frequently absent from the office.

*Julia, private secretary to the deputy chairman and to the group director of Corporate Planning of Heavy Metal*
Julia, like Christine, was in her early forties and had had considerable

experience of secretarial work. She had been in two companies before joining Heavy Metal, where she had spent the past twelve years. Until two years ago she was private secretary to Mr Pearce, who was group director of Corporate Planning. At that time Mr Thole was appointed deputy chairman. As he visited the head office only irregularly and had worked closely with Mr Pearce over the years, the latter suggested that he might ask Julia to help him whenever he needed secretarial assistance. Thus, Julia began working for Mr Thole. However, over the past eighteen months he had been working increasingly at head office, and consequently Julia now found she was spending the equivalent amount of time with each boss. Judging from the remarks made by the other private secretaries at the office, Julia was perceived to be the busiest of them all. Her ability to cope with the work demands stemmed from two factors; first, the co-operative and supportive relationship existing between her two bosses; and secondly, from her own input of effort. Julia always came in at 9.00 a.m. and stayed until 6.00-6.30 p.m.; she never left the office before the departure of both bosses. In addition, unlike Janet and Christine, Julia felt she could not commit herself to a fixed lunch hour.

Since the head office was designed to provide separate private secretarial facilities for both the deputy chairman and group director of Corporate Planning, Julia operated from two offices. Each office was located adjacent to that of the appropriate boss, and were at either end of a corridor, thus it took a few minutes to travel from one office to the other. Her location depended on which boss was coming into the office; each was away about eight weeks in the year. Where both bosses were in Julia divided her day between the two offices. Apparently Mr Thole always came in earlier than Mr Pearce, and consequently after Julia had sorted the incoming mail for both of them she took dictation and any other work from Mr Thole. This did not mean that his work was always given priority; Julia usually evaluated what had to be done during the day for both bosses, and then agreed in advance with each the priority she should give to the various tasks. In this way Julia did not regard either boss as being more important than the other *per se*; instead, the importance of one boss *vis-à-vis* the other was determined on a daily basis. Since Julia was always willing to work late into the evening, she felt that neither boss could complain if she had not completed a particular task that specifically needed to be cleared that day. It appeared that even when the work demands on Julia slackened, for example, when both bosses were absent for an extended period of time, she still worked her usual late hours so that she could 'catch up' on all the filing that accumulated when she was busy.

When either boss was away Julia dealt with his incoming mail and telephone calls wherever possible. On account of Julia's constantly heavy work-loads, she was only able to deal with strictly routine mail and telephone calls; that is, those requiring straightforward information which she had readily at hand. In cases where her judgement was called for she usually undertook the task only after discussing the issue with one of the boss's peers in Heavy Metal. In some situations she directly delegated the task. Such delegation was constrained to the fellow directors at head office. On some occasions when a boss was abroad and she felt that a particular piece of information should be forwarded immediately, she would telephone him to ask whether he wanted it to be telexed to him.

Likewise, when either man was away for more than four days Julia wrote to him, giving a résumé of the incoming information she had received in his absence; and details of how she had dealt with any items, together with a xerox of any letters she regarded as being of particular importance. In this way Julia was able to keep her boss(es) in touch with how she was handling various business matters in their absence.

The latter was an important characteristic of Julia's work pattern. She was much more cautious than the other four secretaries interviewed with respect to her bosses' communications. This seemed to be attributed to two factors. First, she was not as involved in her bosses' work as were the other secretaries (on account of having two bosses), and felt that she did not fully understand the nature of it. Secondly, Julia was a much less self-assured and confident secretary. Her whole approach was typified by 'I had better check with the boss first' rather than making a decision herself with regard to appropriate action.

Over all, Julia appeared to be completely dedicated to her position; this was reflected in the number of hours she worked each day at the office. She exuded a great enthusiasm for her work and showed a high level of respect and personal liking for both her bosses.

### Drawing the interviews together

The outcome of the five interviews described in this chapter cannot be systematically compared since a common set of questions was not applied in each case. This was intentional since I wanted each secretary to generate the issues which she saw as being important in understanding her occupational role. Despite the lack of a common framework for the five interviews, a number of key themes emerged which will now be discussed.

## Type of organization

The nature of the top private secretary's role appeared to vary according to a set of organization structural variables. Type of organization seemed to influence the secretary's activities. Sheila mentioned that she was rarely able to handle any of her boss's letters (head of department) when he was away, since they were frequently concerned with soliciting his opinion on a subject. In contrast, in her previous post in a sales organization she was often able to handle her boss's letters, as many of them were customer queries which tended to be dealt with in a fairly routine way. On the whole, there was less of a sense of urgency surrounding communications in the university, and if her boss was not in the office Sheila rarely delegated issues to subordinates, or undertook them herself. This great difference in the pace of the work and the sense of urgency between the university and the manufacturing company reflected itself in the number of interruptions sustained by the secretaries during the day (far more in the university), and the number of hours put in by the secretaries. (Sheila could always take a fixed lunch hour and rarely stayed beyond the set hours, whereas all the secretaries in Heavy Metal usually worked overtime, and Julia, in particular, could never guarantee her lunch hour.)

## Nature of managerial position

Not only did the type of organization determine in part the secretary's work pattern, but also the managerial position she was attached to within the organization. The functional responsibilities of the boss and his level in the managerial hierarchy greatly influenced the secretary's work. Christine mentioned that working for a marketing director on the board meant that most of her boss's contacts were intra- rather than extra-organizational. When her boss was away for extended periods, she therefore had relatively few communications to deal with, since 90 per cent of her boss's contacts were located within the company and would know of his absence. At chairman level this situation was reversed. Janet estimated that most of her boss's contacts were external, so she made a significant contribution in the handling of communications while he was away. Janet also had far more communications to deal with — certainly twice as many as the marketing director — by virtue of the fact that her boss was chairman, and many outsiders insist on contacting the company at the very top level.

Allied to the factor of the position of the boss within the management hierarchy, is that of his position within other outside organizations. Janet highlighted the public affairs side to her boss's job. He was a member and director of a number of government boards, industrial societies, and school councils; and in the past he had also been a director of other companies. Work derived from these extra-organizational positions was often considerable and inevitably directly affected the secretary's work-load.

## Structure of the boss-secretary relationship

Although at the top level of organizations the traditional boss-private secretary dyadic working relationship prevails, in unusual cases bosses share personal secretaries. This was the situation faced by Julia. As she worked for two high-level bosses she was kept extremely busy. Problems of work priorities, which might otherwise occur, were prevented by the two bosses negotiating the timing of tasks, both with each other and with Julia. Also, Julia made a point of always getting work completed on the requested day, however late it meant working. The nature of Julia's job content was, however, quite different from Janet's. The former seemed to spend a far greater proportion of her time carrying out basic tasks like typing, dictation, opening mail, and answering telephone calls, as a result of looking after two bosses. It meant that she was far less involved than Janet in the 'personal' side of the bosses' work, as well as not getting as deeply involved in the information processing aspect of the job. In addition, Julia's bosses had the time to process much of their own communications because there were less of them, compared to the chairman's, and because there were less demands made upon their time by other people; again, this stands in contrast to the chairman's obligations. It was clear that where a private secretary has two bosses, the composition of her activities is very different from that of a secretary with one boss.

Kerry's position in Heavy Metal illustrated that not only could there be structural options in the number of bosses supported by a secretary, but also on the number of secretaries supporting any one boss. Where there were two private secretaries attached to one boss, as with Janet and Kerry, there was a division of labour with each specializing in different areas. The situation brought out the problems of attempting to break up the secretary's role. Kerry forwarded that all elements of the job were so interconnected that it made no sense to divide them up. It was interesting to note here that while both Janet and Kerry worked directly for the chairman in terms of formal reporting relationships, he would only have personal contact with Janet, thus all messages for Kerry were transmitted through Janet. This made Kerry feel very alienated and did not encourage a good relationship between herself and the chairman; Kerry felt personal contact with the boss was essential in the boss-secretary relationship.

## Physical location in the organization

A fourth factor affecting the private secretary's role is her physical location within the organization. In all cases except that of Kerry, the secretaries' offices were immediately adjacent to those of their bosses. This meant that access to the boss's office could only be made via the secretary's office. Physically, then, the secretary actually operated as a gatekeeper to her boss. There were other important implications to this arrangement. It facilitated the secretary keeping in touch with the boss's activities since invariably the door between the two rooms was left open if the latter was not having a meeting. Therefore, the secretary was automatically in constant touch with the boss's activities. It also meant that the outcome of the boss's meetings — such as the setting up of appointments, passing on of documents, etc. — were easily and quickly communicated to the secretary. There was little likelihood, then, of information being withheld from the secretary, either on an intentional or unintentional basis. Another important facet to the secretary's location was that her office served as a waiting-room for the boss's visitors. This gave the private secretary a unique opportunity to obtain information she might not otherwise have received.

## The nature of the relationship between private secretary and boss

The relationships that these private secretaries had with their bosses were extremely well established in terms of the length of time they had been working together. In the case of Sheila and Janet it was eight and a half and nineteen years respectively; in fact Janet had moved companies with her boss. This phenomenon is interesting in that it suggests that the secretary's primary orientation is to the boss, and not the organization. Bosses have the freedom to hire their own secretaries or 'steal' them when they leave a company. In fact, 'taking the secretary with the boss' is the means whereby many secretaries acquire 'promotion' up the secretarial hierarchy.

The characteristics that emerged in all of these relationships between bosses and private secretaries in both the university and manufacturing company were loyalty, respect, liking, personal commitment, and tremendous involvement. The latter manifested itself in the way private secretaries talked so highly of their bosses' working styles. In Christine's case, she expressed the desire to emulate her boss since she admired him so much. Even where this feeling was not as explicitly voiced, the secretary emphasized how she tried as best she could to please the boss in terms of developing a working style that complemented his. The boss tended to be regarded as the model for the secretary, rather than the secretary imposing her own model of how a secretary should perform. Not one secretary criticized her boss. The commitment and involvement in the job were evidenced by the long hours put in by all the secretaries, sacrificing lunch hours and taking work home. Such extensions to the normal expectations of secretaries are what most separates out the ones in top positions.

### Influence exerted by private secretaries

The influence and discretion top private secretaries exert on their bosses' communications were well brought out in these interviews. All the secretaries (with the exception of Kerry since she was a special case) looked after their bosses' diaries, took all telephone calls, opened the mail, and monitored visitors to their bosses. In particular, Sheila highlighted the importance of her information role to her boss. Janet emphasized that the primary element of her job consisted of being 'an interpreter of her boss's information'. Christine described the way she categorized mail for her boss by placing a priority value on each item, as well as the ways in which she used to help him process it. Julia spoke of the various methods in which she processed incoming information when her bosses were away. In each case the secretary had generated a set of procedures for handling the boss's communication. What was of especial interest emerging from these five interviews was that the key contribution made by each private secretary was quite different. Sheila highlighted her role of supplier of information, Janet her role of processer of mail, Christine her role of allocating her boss's time, and Julia her role of substituting for her bosses in their absence. These variations may be directly attributed to the differences in the bosses' work situations.

### Conclusion

The primary demarcation between top private secretaries and other secretaries in the organization is the nature of the dependency relationship between boss and secretary. Farther down the organization secretaries depend very much upon their bosses; they wait for their bosses to direct their activities, to monitor their work-loads, and to check their work. At the top the situation is reversed, with bosses depending heavily upon their secretaries. Indeed, it is the secretaries who direct their bosses' activities through control of the diary, who monitor their work-load through absorbing the excess, and who check to make sure that their bosses have completed all that they planned to do that day. In the event of the boss being away, the secretary acts as a surrogate for him. Top private secretaries clearly can operate as very effective partners to their bosses.

What particularly emerges from the interviews described in this

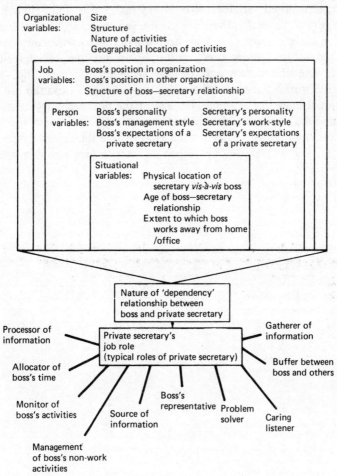

**Fig 3.1** *The main factors influencing the private secretary's job role*

chapter is that the profile of that effective partnership can be very different across boss-secretary relationships. This means that it is impossible to be prescriptive about the effective management of the boss-secretary relationship, in terms of identifying precisely what the private secretary ought to be doing for her boss. The effective management of the relationship is much more related to understanding and complementing each other's needs, strengths, and weaknesses. The value of analysing the five private secretaries in this chapter is that they suggest a number of roles that a private secretary can play, and Figure 3.1 summarizes the main factors influencing this. They are categorized in four ways. The broadest contextual considerations are the organizational variables, like the size, structure, and activities of the company. Secondly, there are the job variables, such as the boss's position in the company, and the structure of the boss-secretary working relationship. Thirdly, there are the person variables, which include aspects like the boss's and private secretary's personalities and preferred working styles; and finally, the last set of variables are the situational ones: for example, the age of the boss-secretary relationship, and the extent to which the boss works away from the office. All these factors interact to delimit the kind of role the private secretary can play. Ten typical roles of the private secretary are also depicted in Figure 3.1.

# 4 | The Context of Top Private Secretarial Work

So far the book has traced the development of the secretarial role, analysed the nature of the secretarial hierarchy, and examined a number of roles private secretaries may be seen to play in organizations. The remainder of the book is devoted to a study (carried out in 1975) of thirty top private secretaries in Great Britain. These private secretaries all worked for managing directors belonging to the largest manufacturing companies. In essence, the study set out to answer three broad questions:

1 Who is a top private secretary?
2 How do you define an effective private secretary?
3 How much influence do top private secretaries exert?

The data were collected by means of in-depth face to face interviews, and a series of questionnaires (see Appendix for research methodology). This chapter will deal with the backgrounds of the top private secretaries, Chapter 5 will examine top private secretaries' definitions of an effective secretary, and Chapter 6 will analyse the actual influence exerted by secretaries in top positions.

### Age

The age range of the sample of top secretaries is shown in Table 4.1 alongside the age range of a cross-section of 515 secretaries in Central London, which formed the basis of another recent study.[1]

What is most striking in the Central London sample is the youthful structure of the secretaries. Over two-thirds of secretaries in Central London are in the age range 20-29; this compares with only 3.0 per cent in the sample of top private secretaries in Britain (in all but four cases they were also based in Central London). In the sample of top secretaries 60 per cent are aged over 40. In fact, the category 40-44

Table 4.1   *Age distribution of top secretaries compared to a cross-section of secretaries*

| Age | Sample of top secretaries (n = 30) | Central London sample (n = 515) |
| --- | --- | --- |
| Under 20 | – | 8% |
| 20–24 | – | 44% |
| 25–29 | 3% | 24% |
| 30–34 | 10% | 5% |
| 35–39 | 27% | 6% |
| 40–44 | 37% | 3% |
| 45–49 | 13% | 4% |
| 50–54 | 7% | 4% |
| 55–59 | 3% | 1% |
| 60–64 | – | 1% |

years is the largest among top secretaries whereas it is 20-24 years which is the largest for the sample of all secretaries in Central London. These points of comparison from Table 4.1 clearly highlight the age differentiation between secretaries in general and top private secretaries. While my sample is very limited, it is evident that top secretaries are not very young; they all had many years of secretarial experience. It is interesting to note, however, that a number of the top secretaries interviewed said that it was becoming much easier for younger secretaries to rise up the hierarchy than it was ten years ago. This is partly because of a shortage of good secretaries, which in turn is due to women today availing themselves of a wider range of career opportunities. The situation has meant that it is now easier for good younger secretaries to reach the top of their career ladder earlier than was traditionally the case. Substantial experience was formerly regarded as a vital qualification for a top position; today it is becoming more usual for it to be an important — but not essential — requirement. These secretaries felt that the decreased significance attributed to experience meant that standards of secretarial work were declining.

Allied to this point is the issue of the status of the top secretary. Today the term 'secretary' embraces anyone with typing skills or typing and shorthand skills. This has resulted in the situation where the majority of secretarial staff in an organization are referred to as 'secretaries'. Formerly they were differentiated by such titles as junior typist, pool typist, shorthand typist, secretary, personal secretary. An explanation of this phenomenon must be found in looking at the changing environment of the secretarial market. Up until the sixties secretarial work was seen as a traditional career for young women. While it retains this popular image, ever increasing numbers of young women are going to university and considering alternative careers. In recent years, this change has been accentuated by the women's liberation movement. The result has been that the market demand for secretaries has outgrown the market supply of them, and agencies offering the services of temporary secretaries profitably developed to meet this imbalance. They were able to offer stopgap services to companies as well as helping them to recruit new permanent secretaries. An important attraction of secretarial agencies was that they were able to provide opportunities for employment to secretaries wanting to work irregular hours.

There were also a number of detrimental repercussions of these 'temp agencies'. In order to make the jobs appear attractive the agencies 'upmarketed' the jobs, such that even the most lowly copy typist became a 'secretary'. Job titles thus became virtually meaningless and top secretaries were deprived of the high status they had previously held. Secondly, because of the insecurity of the 'temp', rates of pay were relatively high. This meant that frequently a 'temp' working alongside a permanent secretary was earning much more than her, which could cause a great deal of friction among the permanent employees in the company. Finally, 'temp agencies' allowed 'secretaries' to hop from job to job, thus giving them the opportunity to 'try out' different companies. Many permanent secretaries have obtained their jobs via a 'temp' experience. Secretaries no longer had to tolerate job dissatisfaction; the easy alternative was to become a 'temp'. The availability of this option to secretaries has put some pressure on management to improve the design of the secretary's job if they wish to retain their permanent secretarial staff. In many companies the employment of 'temps' is an expensive and inefficient way of using secretarial staff. It is apparent that a number of companies are sensitive to this problem and a few are taking some action concerning it.

The lack of status attached to top secretarial work had prompted a number of the secretaries interviewed into requesting a change of job title. Several had asked to be called 'executive secretaries' or 'personal assistants'. There was, however, some resistance to this move by other personnel, particularly in relation to the term 'personal assistant'.

## Length of service

The most striking feature of Table 4.2 is the considerable length of time top private secretaries have been in their organizations. The

Table 4.2   *Length of service of top private secretaries*

| Number of years | 1−5 yrs | 6−10 yrs | 11−15 yrs | 16−20 yrs | Over 20 yrs |
|---|---|---|---|---|---|
| Breakdown of sample | 24% | 10% | 24% | 14% | 28% |

average (defined as the mode) is over twenty years. In typical cases the women had entered the company via the typing pool and had gradually worked their way up to the 'executive' level. This observation is consistent with the older top secretaries' perceptions, that is, that experience in the company used to be essential in rising up the secretarial ladder. Whether this substantial grounding in secretarial work reflects itself in more effective performance is difficult to assess, owing to the subjective criteria defining effective secretarial performance. In turn, this revolves around the whole issue of the differing expectations managers have of their secretaries. Effective secretarial performance is much more a case of the degree to which the secretary's working style complements that of her manager. Thus a secretary's working style is not a mirror reflection of her manager's. It is more a case of balancing one style against the other, such that the secretary can compensate for her boss's weaknesses and highlight his strengths. In sum, they should work as a fully integrated team.

While it may be extremely difficult to evaluate whether top private secretaries who have spent longer with their companies are more effective than top private secretaries who have been recruited from 'outside', the top private secretaries who have spent over ten years with their companies see strong attractions allied to their positions.

1  The secretary is very familiar with the nature of the organization, in terms of its structure, personnel, products, markets, and customers. When one considers that all the companies making up the sample employed in this study were multi-national and trading on an international basis with a huge variety of products, then this factor assumes great importance.

2  Staying with one organization for a long period of time can encourage greater personal commitment and work motivation. The latter may be illustrated in terms of the concept of 'creeping commitment'. The longer one stays in an organization, receiving regular promotions, so there may be a tendency to see the development of an enduring and satisfying reciprocal relationship.

3  Progressing to the top via experience in a variety of divisions,

departments, levels, and bosses, means that the secretary builds up a tremendous first-hand knowledge and understanding of the problems and issues that occur at all levels in the organization. This means she has a good understanding of the background of problems and issues dealt with at the executive level.

4 Progressing to the top either via a total working experience with one boss (as was the case with several secretaries) or with a variety of bosses, means that the secretary has forged a number of personal relationships throughout the organization. This is invaluable in her role at the top where one interacts with the organization on such a global scale.

5 In the situation where a 'new' boss inherits an 'old' secretary (a frequent occurrence at managing director/chief executive/chairman level), the secretary can operate as an effective, albeit often unofficial, tool in the induction process. This is particularly true where the boss is recruited from 'outside'. The secretary has the knowledge, and indeed may have lived through many significant historical events in the company. She is familiar with company procedures and practices and knows how the last boss managed the role and what his specific problem was. Where the secretary is asked to play this 'training' function, she must do so very delicately since she must not try to foist or impose her last boss's working style on her current boss. Again, this underlines the point made earlier that essentially the secretary's role must be defined in conjunction with the manager's role.

The above five factors are extremely important in understanding the potential influence exerted by the top secretary. They highlight the tremendous fund of 'esoteric organizational knowledge' that top secretaries may develop in the course of moving up through the company and through different managers. What is so special about this knowledge is that it is only possessed by the private secretary and not by her boss. This gives the secretary a potential power basis on which to operate in her job, that is, she has information that her boss needs.

In contrast to the majority of the sample who had been with the company for over ten years, two of the secretaries had recently (in the last four years) been recruited from outside, thus having none of the above advantages. One of these secretaries said that her boss had advertised the post in the national newspapers because he wanted someone with 'no personal alliances in the organization'. This sentiment brings out the recognition of the potential influence a top private secretary can bring to bear, and allied to this, the danger that this influence may be channelled to counter the boss's position, an acknowledgement of the political power that may accrue for the alert secretary.

When the other 'outside' secretary was being considered for her current position, she was interviewed by all the other board secretaries. This secretarial participation in what is traditionally seen as one manager's decision took place in order to encourage good feelings and acceptance of the new employee. The benefits gained from this piece of foresight were emphasized by the secretary involved. She described how the other top secretaries went out of their way to help her in the early months. This meant that she was quickly known and accepted by everyone, and that if ever she had a work problem there was always someone to whom she could easily turn for help. This smooth integration into the company, and particularly into the secretarial side, is extremely important, since most of a top private secretary's time is spent in negotiation and co-ordination with the other secretaries. In contrast, in one of the other organizations studied, the managing director, who had himself come in as an 'outsider', imported his secretary with him. No attempt was made to introduce her to the other secretaries before his appointment. This secretary recalled the bitter resentment that evolved among the other board secretaries, which manifested itself in terms of being cold, detached, and uncooperative towards her. She said that it took her at least six months before she felt fully integrated into the company. She rationalized this secretarial reaction in terms of the aura, prestige, and status attached to the top secretarial post in an organization. In addition, this particular position traditionally goes to a secretary who has worked within the company for a number of years — a reward for loyalty and talent. That it went to an outsider meant that the other secretaries in the company felt deprived as well as resentful at being overlooked in the situation.

## Length of experience with current manager

Length of experience with current manager varied from one and a half to twenty-three years. Nearly half the secretaries had been with their bosses over five years and 20 per cent had been with them for over ten (see Table 4.3). It is interesting to note here that the three secretaries who had been working with their bosses for over twenty years had all seen their bosses receive O.B.E.s for their services to industry. In the fourth case of a boss receiving the O.B.E. his secretary had been with

Table 4.3 *Length of experience with current manager*

| Number of years | 1–5 yrs | 6–10 yrs | 11–15 yrs | 16–20 yrs | Over 20 yrs |
|---|---|---|---|---|---|
| Breakdown of sample | 53% | 27% | 10% | – | 10% |

him for twelve years. In all four situations the secretaries impressed upon me how active their bosses were in other organizations and government bodies. The extra-organizational demands directly affected the respective secretaries' work-loads. Each of the four involved herself heavily in these activities: arranging meetings, preparing minutes, briefing her boss, and frequently personally attending social functions allied to these activities. An enormous amount of time can be invested by the secretary in such events. One private secretary interviewed, whose boss had a number of such commitments, had an assistant whose sole function was to liaise with her boss's wife about such events, since the latter was invariably included in the arrangements.

Although data on salary was not systematically collected,[2] the secretary with twenty years of experience with her boss apparently emerged as being the highest paid secretary in Britain, according to a survey conducted at the time of this study. Her salary approximated £6,000. At the time of being interviewed this secretary was deliberating over whether she would move with her boss when he took over the chairmanship of a large nationalized industry in six months' time. The major problems were that the new company would be unable to integrate her current salary into its over-all secretarial reward policies, and that she would forfeit the tremendous financial benefits derived from the pension scheme attached to her current company. In order to meet this problem her boss had offered to make up her salary personally from his own, so that she could keep apace with her current earning scale. This example gives some indication of the dependence of this boss upon his private secretary, and his reluctance to lose her. It also prompts discussion of perks for top private secretaries. In general, there was a noticeable lack of them. Some secretaries, in common with top managers, were allocated parking spaces at the company. In only one company was the private secretary given a car, although other secretaries were frequently given transport and meal allowances when they worked late. Only one of the secretaries had her own expense account, and this was the secretary whose boss was so reluctant to lose her. Over all, then, the picture of the secretary is one in which very little formal recognition and reward is given by the organization for conscientious performance. Where recognition and rewards are given they tend to come directly from the manager, thus reinforcing the perception that the secretary works primarily for the boss and not the organization.

## Context of the private secretary's work situation: hours worked

As can be seen in Table 4.4, the hours worked each day varied from seven to eleven hours. These statistics were derived from times of arrival and departure, discounting one hour for lunch. In many cases that hour is worked. In addition, a number of the secretaries reported working beyond these hours when required. Week-end work was very occasionally undertaken and certain secretaries were also expected to attend a number of social functions outside of office hours. Hence the profile presented in Table 4.4 is a very conservative one. What immediately emerges from it is that on the basis that a normal working

Table 4.4   *Numbers of hours worked on average each day by the top private secretaries*

| Number of hours worked each day | 7–8 hrs | 8–9 hrs | 9–10 hrs | 10–11 hrs | Over 11 hours |
|---|---|---|---|---|---|
| Breakdown of sample | 29% | 43% | 21% | 4% | 3% |

day is seven hours (allowing an hour for lunch), all the top private secretaries in this sample work an extended day, some considerably longer than others. All the secretaries, when interviewed on this, said that the pressures and demands made upon them meant that unless they voluntarily put in the extra hours the work would never be completed. In addition, this pressure is fairly constantly applied throughout the year so there is no opportunity for secretaries 'to let go'. A further pressure is that the boss's role and its fulfilment is highly visible and initiatory, and this productive quality must be to some extent absorbed by the secretary.

In all but one case the secretaries arrived at the office very early in the morning and virtually always before the bosses. This meant that the secretary could have the mail opened, sorted, and items requiring his attention ready for him. Bosses usually liked this arrangement, and indeed, in most cases, insisted upon it. One secretary described how, if she was as much as five minutes late in the morning, her boss might refuse to talk to her for several hours. Another secretary explained how her boss had taken an even more extreme position. One day she was ten minutes late at the office, arriving at 8.40 a.m., instead of her usual 8.30 a.m. The boss's reprisal was to arrange a company chauffeur to pick her up each morning at 8.00 a.m. in order to guarantee her early arrival. This practice has now existed for several years. While this anecdote can be appreciated ironically (that the secretary's punishment turned out to be a valuable company perk), it does also illustrate the expense that the boss felt was warranted in order to ensure that his secretary arrived early at the office.

Without exception, the secretaries revealed themselves to be extremely conscientious in their work, taking the long hours as a matter of course. 'The pressures in this job are fantastic. You can certainly rule out any social life, because you can't rely on getting away in the evenings.'

Several of the secretaries did stress how much it jeopardized social and family life, but they were all confident about the particular career decisions they had made. In one situation the private secretary completely dedicated herself to her work. She normally worked from 8.00 a.m. to 8.00 p.m. and when exceptional events occurred, for example annual company conferences, industrial disputes causing production stoppages, she might work late into the night and had been known to work through to the early hours of the morning — 6.00 a.m. being quoted here. This particular secretary would also work occasionally at the week-ends. This exceptional secretary worked for an American company and had an American boss. Unfortunately, since he was the only American boss in the sample it was impossible to test the hypothesis that number of hours worked each day varied with the cultural background of the boss. This observation is, however, consistent with the traditional perception of American management being more highly motivated and working longer hours than its British counterparts.

On the issue of hours worked by secretaries, it is worth mentioning that in one organization visited flexi-time was introduced on an experimental basis, but was quickly withdrawn as a system which was not viable for top secretaries. The results emerging from the experiment showed that the top secretaries were regularly putting in an average of two to three days a month over and above their designated hours of employment. The system was also unable to cope with the idiosyncratic and heavy demands made upon top secretaries.

## Structure of the top private secretary's job position

Probably the most significant finding here is that 27 per cent of the secretaries have full-time secretarial assistance (see Table 4.5). In each

Table 4.5 *Structure of the top private secretary's job position*

| Types of structural positions | Breakdown of sample (%) |
| --- | --- |
| Boss/Board has male personal assistant | 10 |
| Has full-time secretarial assistance | 27 |
| Has part-time secretarial assistance | 3 |
| Operates entirely on own | 60 |

case, the situation was described as the boss having two secretaries: one, a senior private secretary/personal assistant; and the other, a junior secretary. However, apart from two organizations, all the private secretaries in this category (i.e. 75 per cent) emphasized that they alone, and never the junior secretaries, handled ongoing personal contacts with their bosses. This is at the insistence of the bosses. The junior secretaries thus received their work instructions from their more senior 'partners'. Therefore it would be more accurate to describe the junior secretaries as subordinates of the private secretaries and two levels down from the boss. In the other two organizations somewhat unusual working situations had evolved, which are worth elaborating on here. In both companies the two secretaries reported directly to the managing director. In one of the organizations each of the secretaries had a particular area of the boss's activities to look after; these were very broadly broken down into domestic (British) business and overseas business. There was, however, a distinct difference in age and status between the two secretaries, one was in her early twenties, while the other was in her mid-thirties, and the older one clearly had primary responsibility and accountability for all the secretarial activities carried out in the office. She also had more contact with the boss and more responsible tasks to carry out. Included in the latter was the monthly duty of writing the managing director's report to the board. This usually took four days to complete and involved obtaining reports from all fourteen subsidiary companies, reading them, abstracting the salient points, checking figures, and then collating it all and 'presenting it in an easy and interesting form'.

In the second company again both secretaries reported directly to the managing director but the tasks were divided up rather differently. Some years ago the managing director had only one private secretary. During that time a particularly important industrial dispute arose in one of the company's factories. Since the boss was keen to find out locally what was happening but did not want to get involved personally at that stage, he asked his private secretary to find out what she could about the situation. The result was that the local plant manager 'opened up' to the secretary and gave her a great deal of useful information. The managing director was so delighted with the result that he extended his secretary's 'information seeking' role, so that now this secretary spends a great proportion of her time putting together situation reports for her boss. This is less to indicate that the secretary can perform a 'spy' role but more to acknowledge that she may be more approachable and even understanding than her boss. This extension to her role meant that she had less time to do the traditional secretarial tasks, thus when the managing directorship moved from one man to the new incumbent, the latter maintained his predecessor's secretary as well as his own. Hence there is now one secretary who performs primarily personal assistant-type tasks and the other who is a private secretary, in the more traditional sense of the word.

## Amount of time devoted to boss's personal business

The work a private secretary undertakes for her boss derives from two sources. One is the intra-organizational initiated work, that is, work derived from the boss's position as managing director of the company. The other is the extra-organizational work, and this in turn comes primarily from two sources: one is the other organizations that the manager is a director or member of, and the other is the personal activities of the man. The latter cover a range of communications from the routine to the non-routine, for example, from paying his Diners Club Card and looking after his bank statements, to handling the legal and administrative aspects of purchasing a house or stocks and shares on his behalf. These are classed together as personal business because they relate to his personal life-style and not to his work activities. Time devoted to carrying out work allied to the boss's personal affairs varied from 2 per cent to 90 per cent (see Table 4.6). On the whole, those secretaries who had been with their bosses longest spent more time doing personal work. Perhaps the amount of personal work a secretary undertakes for her boss is a useful indication

Table 4.6 *Amount of time devoted to boss's personal business*

| Amount of time devoted to personal business | 1–10% | 11–20% | 21–30% | 31–40% | Over 40% |
|---|---|---|---|---|---|
| Breakdown of sample | 40% | 20% | 7% | 17% | 16% |

of the degree of involvement and personal commitment she has with her boss as an individual, and not just as a member of the organization. Personal work demands may be seen as a purely discretionary element of a secretary's job; that is to say, it is entirely up to the secretary as to whether she decides to undertake work of this nature for her boss. The carrying out of personal work is not officially seen as part of the secretary's job role.

Such a rational interpretation, however, is too simplistic and does not reflect the reality of the situation. The role of the private secretary in the organization is unique in that it is totally defined around one person: the parallel manager. It is the manager who primarily defines the parameters of the role and evaluates the incumbent's performance. The functions carried out by the secretary in any specific boss-secretary relationship are the result of a kind of negotiation process between the two respective individuals, with the manager having the ultimate power in that he can hire and fire her. Again, this indicates the process whereby the secretary works primarily for the man and not the organization. An analysis of the derivation of a top private secretary's work endorses this situation. It is not unusual for a secretary to spend 20 per cent of her time on personal business allied to the running of his non-work oriented duties, 30 per cent on business related to the manager's position in other organizations, and the remaining 50 per cent on business allied to his position as full-time managing director.

A measure of the amount of time a secretary devotes to the manager's personal business is significant since it indicates the nature of the relationship between herself and her manager. The longer they have been working together the easier it is for a boss to allocate personal tasks to her. Over time the trust, loyalty, and discretion which the private secretary may have evolved for her boss will also have increased, such that the boss feels confident (and not guilty) about giving his secretary such tasks. The hypothesis that the longer a secretary has worked with the manager the more likely it is that she will spend a greater amount of time on his personal business, was empirically tested and upheld in this study (see Table 4.7).

In all cases in the sample the secretaries were quick to point out that personal work had a lower priority than company work. At the same time all the secretaries were extremely conscientious, thus rather than it being a case of personal business not being carried out by them it was merely completed after company work. One secretary in the sample was quite exceptional in relation to the amount of time spent on personal business; she estimated that over 90 per cent of her time

Table 4.7 *Length of time with boss and amount of time devoted to personal business*

| Amount of time spent on personal business | Length of time with boss 5 years and under | 6 years and over | Total |
|---|---|---|---|
| 1–20 per cent of time | 14 | 4 | 18 |
| Over 20 per cent of time | 3 | 9 | 12 |
| *Total* | *17* | *13* | |

*Note:* Formula for estimating $\chi^2$:

$$= \frac{N(1\ AD - BC\ 1 - \frac{N}{2})^2}{(A+B)\ (C+D)\ (A+C)\ (B+D)}\ df = 1$$

(See Siegal, S., *Non Parametric Statistics for the Behavioural Sciences*, McGraw-Hill, 1965, p. 107.)

$$\chi^2 = 6.159 \quad df = 1 \quad p < .01$$

was tied up in this way. This secretary spoke of the very conservative attitudes held towards secretaries in the company. It was only in the last ten years that any members of the board had been allocated a private secretary. Consequently she felt that board members, like her boss, had not yet really learned how to use a private secretary, since they were used to working with male personal assistants. In this particular situation the term 'office wife' took on an even greater meaning than usual, as the secretary was almost totally concerned with 'home based' matters.

## Amount of time boss is absent from office

The boss's location is an important factor influencing the private secretary's job activities. If the boss is always accessible, the private secretary can always refer any problems to him. However, if he spends extensive periods of time on external meetings, both overseas and within Great Britain, then this may give the private secretary greater responsibility in running the office when he is absent.

Table 4.8 *Amount of time boss is absent from the organization*

| Percentage of time | 1–10% | 11–20% | 21–30% | 31–40% | 41–50% | Over 50% |
|---|---|---|---|---|---|---|
| Breakdown of sample | 0% | 15% | 23% | 31% | 23% | 8% |

As can be seen in Table 4.8, over 60 per cent of the sample have bosses who are absent from their offices for over 30 per cent of the time. Two of the secretaries in the highest category had bosses who spent 60 per cent and 70 per cent of the time away from their organizational bases. This kind of situation clearly encouraged the secretary to take an active role in the organization in terms of handling her boss's communication network.

These periods of time spent away vary from being a trip of a few days visiting operational units within Britain or Europe, to consisting of a trip of six weeks, which might involve a number of conferences and annual policy meetings around the world. Most bosses do not like to be away longer than three weeks so the extended trip of six weeks is very much the exception. Trips to Europe, however, are a frequent occurrence. One boss spent one week each month in the Brussels office. His private secretary was quite exceptional in that she used to accompany him for three of the five days every month. Thus she had two offices. The advantage of this arrangement was that the secretary could handle all the boss's work rather than the latter being divided up between two secretaries. On the whole, most secretaries did not accompany their bosses overseas, although several visited factories, and attended meetings with them within Britain. The managing director of a major car company situated in Coventry spent quite a lot of time in London. If he had to be away for more than several days he would ask his secretary to come with him for one or two of those days. She said that they could get through a lot of work in the car while being chauffeured to London, since the car was fitted with a telephone.

When bosses did go away for lengthy trips they depended, as they usually did, on their secretaries preparing all the papers and gathering all the information they needed. Here the secretary must anticipate her boss's needs: 'The role of being a supplier of information is very important; if I forget anything then he just has to go without it because he usually doesn't have time to check everything before leaving.'

Some of the secretaries felt that life was much easier in the boss's absence since there was no one there to initiate work; however, this by no means implied that they had nothing to do. Filing tended to get done during such times, and while the boss is away the private secretary can be asked by other directors' secretaries to help or even advise them. This may include asking for advice on what the absent boss would think of a new development or how he would react to an unexpected occurrence. On the whole, the primary task of the secretary is to keep the communications flowing; she cannot allow papers to mount up on her boss's desk so this involves dealing with them herself, dealing with them in consultation with other directors, or totally delegating them. In one organization this decision was taken out of the secretary's hands; when the managing director was away the role was rotated among the other directors. In this situation, then, the private secretary had to liaise closely with the respective director in terms of keeping notes of all his actions. Even then, it was the secretary who decided what should be kept back for the boss to acknowledge. Some secretaries felt they were capable of handling far more decisions than they did: 'I can't make decisions in his absence although in some cases I would certainly feel confident at doing so.'

One secretary pointed out that many decisions occurring at the top could easily await the boss's return — unless he was away for a very long trip: 'Lower down decisions are mainly operational so it is important that they be taken immediately; at the top they are mainly policy so they can usually await the return of the boss.'

## Conclusion

In general, the picture that emerges in this chapter is one in which top private secretaries are not young (average: 40 to 44 years of age); have a substantial base of secretarial experience (over twenty years), which is gained primarily with one company and often with one boss; and work very long days (eight to nine hours) (see Figure 4.1). There were indications, however, that the typical career profile of top private secretaries is changing.

Although there were not many young secretaries in my sample (only 13 per cent were aged under 34), their background experience had been gained from a relatively frequent change of jobs with a number of companies. This 'job hopping', they felt, had accelerated their rise to the top of the secretarial hierarchy. They speculated that had they stayed in their original companies and relied on internal promotion, they would not have reached such a high level so early in their careers. These individuals believed strongly that if a secretary wants to be successful she must take a high degree of responsibility in planning her personal growth and career development. She must be proactive in moving herself up the secretarial hierarchy. Secretaries should not forget that bosses may face a dilemma in interests when appraising their secretaries' performance and evaluating their prospects for promotion. If a secretary is efficient then a boss will not want to lose her. This will certainly bias his annual appraisal of her. It is only fair to add here that it is not just bosses who are reluctant to change

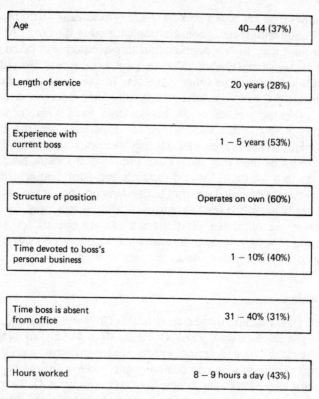

| | |
|---|---|
| Age | 40—44 (37%) |
| Length of service | 20 years (28%) |
| Experience with current boss | 1 – 5 years (53%) |
| Structure of position | Operates on own (60%) |
| Time devoted to boss's personal business | 1 – 10% (40%) |
| Time boss is absent from office | 31 – 40% (31%) |
| Hours worked | 8 – 9 hours a day (43%) |

**Fig 4.1** *Profile of a top private secretary*

secretaries. Such job inertia is also likely to affect a number of secretaries, their defence being that it is so difficult to establish a good working relationship with a boss, and that having done so they are wary of breaking it. This job inertia, which can jeopardize the secretary's career and encourage the boss to become rigid in his expectations of her, will only start to be alleviated when bosses understand how to use secretaries efficiently. Certainly if this trend of secretaries becoming more active in determining their careers continues, then inevitably it will put more pressure on companies to respond to secretarial needs with respect to career development.

If there is a trend among younger secretaries to move relatively quickly from one company to another, then there is the opposite tendency among older secretaries, who tend to stay with the company and with one boss. It is also interesting to add that in the situation of the boss leaving the company for a different job, and the secretary having the choice of leaving also after many years to follow him, or conversely, leaving him after many years to stay with the company, she will invariably choose the former strategy. Again this reinforces the belief that the secretary's primary commitment is to the boss and not the organization. This practice reinforces the secretary's career dependence on her boss, and the boss's work dependence upon his secretary.

Why does this practice persist? From the secretary's point of view she is faced with the uncertainty of a new boss. In addition, there is usually the positive lure of an increased salary from the boss's new company who want her to move with him. If the latter is the main reason it may be short-sighted of the secretary to accept the offer. She may be merely putting off the time when she will have to leave her boss (assuming that he is at director level, he may be nearing retirement). If this situation occurs only a few years after moving to the new company, she may be much worse off than if it had occurred in the original organization. Long years of service may encourage a much more caring attitude from the company towards such a secretary.

On the other hand, if the private secretary chooses to leave her company through her boss's change of jobs, her company may not be too upset. The problem of finding another boss for her has been avoided, and there may be substantial financial savings for them in terms of her future pension. The new organization accepts her because she is part of the negotiation process whereby they acquire her boss. In other words, the new company may view the private secretary in almost purely instrumental terms. All factors considered, if the private secretary is asked to move companies with her boss, she should carefully analyse the motives at play. In particular, she should look at the possible long-term repercussions of such a career move: she may risk the situation of being 'left on the shelf'.

# 5 | Defining an Effective Private Secretary

The objective of this chapter is to explore how top private secretaries define an effective private secretary and how they relate themselves to this profile. However, before examining these findings it is useful to step back and conceptualize the kind of role the top private secretary fulfils in an organization. As has already been indicated in previous chapters, her significance links up closely with the influence she is able to bring to bear in her boss's communication systems. The basis of the private secretary's influence lies in the nature of her gatekeeper position: sitting at the junction of all the boss's communications — visitors, telephone calls, and mail, and having control over them. The physical location of the private secretary's office *vis-à-vis* her boss serves to emphasize her gatekeeper position. In the great majority of cases in my study, the private secretary's office was immediately adjacent to that of her boss's. Entrance to the boss's office was therefore only possible via the private secretary's office.

How does the private secretary exert influence in the gatekeeper position? Such an explanation initially requires a definition of the word 'influence'. Without referring to the literature in depth here, let us accept the basic definition that it is 'the process whereby A modifies the attitudes or behaviour of B'.[1] If the private secretary does exert influence, it is necessary to demonstrate that the boss will change his attitudes towards the information, or process the information differently (for example, alter his decision) as a result of the private secretary's intervention. Influence, then, refers here to the difference between the flow of information *as it occurs* and *as it would occur* if it bypassed the private secretary. It therefore refers to any kind of action the private secretary takes to change the nature of the information.

Social psychological theory indicates that attitude change may be induced by a number of factors related to the information; namely, the form/medium, the actual contents, the timing, and the way the contents are presented. (The latter refers to the language used and the way the contacts are structured.) Two other key influences affecting one's attitude towards information are the situational factors, and the characteristics of the communicator.[2] These factors are illustrated in Figure 5.1.

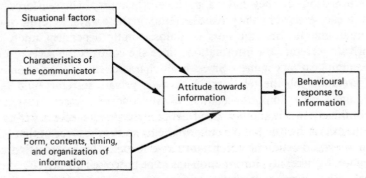

**Fig 5.1** *Factors affecting attitudes towards information*

These components must now be examined in relation to the private secretary's role (see Figure 5.2). My study aimed to measure the influence exerted by the private secretary on the form, contents, timing, and organization of the various communications to the boss. It is important, then, to consider whether the situational factors and

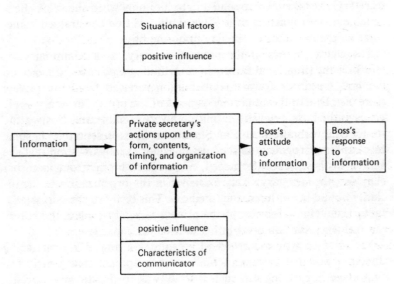

**Fig 5.2** *Factors affecting boss's attitude and behaviour towards information*

the characteristics of the communicator (the private secretary) are likely to have a positive or negative influence on the boss's attitude towards information received from the private secretary. If they have a negative effect they then counteract the influence of the private secretary over the form, contents, timing, and organization of the information. If they have a positive effect they will reinforce the influence exerted by the private secretary in these ways. In terms of the situational factors, the boss is almost totally dependent upon the private secretary for information, since she controls the access to his communication channels. Since this is characteristic of the top private secretary's job the relationship between private secretary and boss assumes great importance; it is usually one of respect, trust, and confidence in one another. Confidence in the private secretary to carry out tasks as he (the boss) would do them, must exist since at that level in the organization he is constantly overloaded with information and hence, by necessity, information has to be processed quickly. The boss rarely has time to check the private secretary's activities. An allied aspect to the situational factors is that over time the private secretary learns the boss's moods and behavioural responses to the point where she can accurately predict his reaction to almost any given situation. Thus, in terms of deciding when to send information to him, one of the factors affecting her choice of time is her gauging of his mood. When problematic information has to be managed by the private secretary, she takes care to send it in to him only when she thinks he is capable of best reacting to it. This timing will be constrained somewhat by the demands of the day upon the boss.

The characteristics of the private secretary, as a communicator, reinforce the situational factors in contributing a positive influence on the boss's attitude towards information received from the private secretary. Due to the situational aspects of the private secretary's role *vis-à-vis* the boss, she is by definition a very credible and trustworthy source of information for him. She acts as his representative, in some cases as his surrogate, and the boss does not usually question that she acts in his best interests. Indeed, as has been brought out in earlier chapters, the secretary's very existence in the organization is significantly bound up with pleasing the boss. This being so, the situational factors and characteristics of the private secretary explain the potential influence she can exert in her gatekeeper capacity.

My research was concerned with examining how thirty managing directors' private secretaries actually used this potential influence. The first stage in carrying out such a study was to decide what specific secretarial activities would be focused on. The character of the

communication media was an obvious starting-point and thus suggested looking at how private secretaries dealt with:

1 Mail.
2 Telephone calls.
3 Personal visitors.
4 Arranging the boss's diary.

While the last two overlap, since most visitors make appointments
before seeing the managing director, some people do not and instead
make these appointments directly with the boss; thus the private
secretary will only handle the actual meeting with the visitor. Outside
of these four basic areas of communication activity three others
seemed to be important. The private secretary acts as her own
information gatherer on the basis of her own contacts in the organization. This is particularly important where she has worked in the
company for a number of years. This can, therefore, constitute a
useful channel of information to the boss.

Private secretaries may spend quite a lot of time with their bosses,
discussing and resolving issues together. In other words, boss and
private secretary jointly decide what action should be taken. It is
difficult to separate out precisely how much influence the private
secretary exerts in this situation, but in terms of appreciating her
influence it is important to know to what extent she is brought into
such consultative discussions.

The last area to consider was not a type of communication but a
kind of situation. At the highest level in the organization the boss
invariably has to spend considerable periods of time away from base.
If the boss no longer exists as an immediate next link in the communication system what does the private secretary do? This is a particular
type of organizational contingency situation (but by no means unusual
as evidenced in the previous chapter) that the private secretary
operates in. At either extreme the boss can either nominate a
managerial substitute who will totally operate on his behalf, or he can
let his private secretary act as his surrogate. In the case of the latter,
she will clearly wield more influence, or at least have more potential
to wield, than when her boss is present. However the individual
boss-private secretary dyad cope with this contingency (managing
the boss's absence), it does represent the situation where the private secretary potentially has maximum influence. The seven areas
of communication activity that were examined were therefore as
follows:

1 Mail.
2 Telephone.
3 Personal visitors.
4 Diary.
5 The private secretary as a channel of information in her own right.
6 Support activities provided by the private secretary.
7 The situation where the boss is absent.

In the case of the first three areas, information is channelled to the private secretary, and she must decide how she is going to process and subsequently transmit it to her boss. In each of these cases a range of actions is open to her which may be arranged into a kind of taxonomy in terms of degrees of influence exerted by the private secretary. These are outlined in the model shown in Figure 5.3.

The model illustrates how information is acted upon by the private secretary. It is based on the observations and comments made in the early stages of the fieldwork. Essentially it shows the different options open to the private secretary in relation to each communication activity. In some cases this results in the information not reaching the boss at all, for example, where the private secretary handles it on her own or redirects it to another director. In other situations it results in the private secretary partly influencing it, perhaps by drafting a reply to a letter which is then passed through to the boss for his approval. In cases of least involvement by the secretary, it results in her passing through the information in exactly the same format as it was received by her; in other words, no influence has been exerted on the contents of the communication. The timing of it, however, may have been affected, and this is important since it may critically alter the managing director's response. A measure of how private secretaries affect the timing and sequence of information was therefore also obtained in the study.

## The results

An attitude scale, consisting of forty-eight statements describing the various activities of private secretaries in these seven areas, was used to ascertain ideal and actual profiles of the thirty top private secretaries. Each of the thirty secretaries was asked first to respond to the forty-eight statements in terms of how they described her idea of an effective private secretary, and then in terms of how they described her own activities.

For example, responses to the statement 'The private secretary

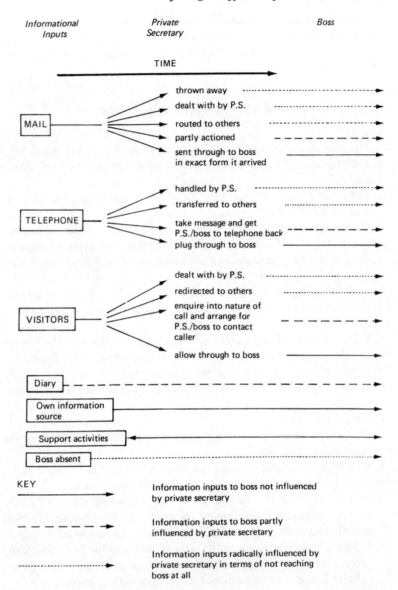

Informational Inputs | Private Secretary | Boss

TIME

MAIL
- thrown away
- dealt with by P.S.
- routed to others
- partly actioned
- sent through to boss in exact form it arrived

TELEPHONE
- handled by P.S.
- transferred to others
- take message and get P.S./boss to telephone back
- plug through to boss

VISITORS
- dealt with by P.S.
- redirected to others
- enquire into nature of call and arrange for P.S./boss to contact caller
- allow through to boss

Diary

Own information source

Support activities

Boss absent

KEY

⟶ Information inputs to boss not influenced by private secretary

⟶ Information inputs to boss partly influenced by private secretary

⟶ Information inputs radically influenced by private secretary in terms of not reaching boss at all

**Fig 5.3** *A model of how the private secretary affects the boss's information*

maintains complete control over her boss's diary' fell into four categories: general practice, sometimes occurs, rarely occurs, never occurs? These responses were scored 4, 3, 2 and 1 respectively. Total scores for each individual theoretically ranged from 48 to 152 and for each item (= statement) from 30 to 120.

Those forty-eight statements are as follows. It is useful to study them both in terms of providing clarity to the discussion of the results in this chapter, and in terms of examining the reader's own use of his/her secretary.

## The various facets of a private secretary's job role

### Diary

1  The private secretary always knows the location of her boss.
2  The private secretary maintains complete control over her boss's diary.
3  The private secretary exercises discretion in setting up appointments and meetings for her boss.
4  Where the boss is required to attend a meeting at a time when he/she is scheduled for another appointment the private secretary decides whether to rearrange the programme and how this should be done.
5  Each morning the private secretary gives her boss a plan of his/her appointments for the day, together with any relevant background notes to them.
6  When outside colleagues/clients/suppliers visit the boss the private secretary makes all the administrative arrangements for them.
7  Where a visitor extends the meeting the private secretary decides whether to remind the boss discreetly of his/her next appointment.

### Personal visitors

1  The private secretary carefully screens all the *ad hoc* visitors to the boss throughout the day.
2  Where the nature of the visit is a routine enquiry the private secretary answers it herself, thereby saving her boss's time.
3  Where the nature of the visit is one involving the release of confidential information the private secretary decides whether the boss would want such information passed on to the particular enquirer.
4  Where a subordinate wishes to refer an issue to the boss which the private secretary feels should be dealt with at a lower level, she tactfully redirects that subordinate to an appropriate person.
5  The private secretary is specifically approached by the boss's peers/subordinates as a sounding-board for ideas since she is able to bring her boss's perspective to the issue.
6  Where a boss's peer/subordinate comes to discuss an issue with him/her but discovers that the boss is unavailable, the private secretary will attempt to gain as much information from the person as is necessary for the boss to take action on it as soon as possible.

7 Where an *ad hoc* visitor sees the boss the private secretary will brief the boss on the nature of the visit and provide him/her with any necessary files/notes before the meeting.

*Support activities*
1 The private secretary helps the boss in planning his/her various work programmes.
2 The private secretary discusses work procedures with the boss and suggests improvements where necessary.
3 Where the boss delegates work to a peer/subordinate, he/she leaves the arranging of this to his/her private secretary.
4 Where the boss assigns a work programme to members of management, he/she delegates the supervision of this to his/her private secretary.
5 If the boss is unable to attend a meeting, the private secretary represents him/her.
6 Where the boss is very occupied, the private secretary entertains guests/clients on his/her behalf.
7 The private secretary encourages the development of good communications between the boss and all external and internal personnel.

*The private secretary as a source of information*
1 The private secretary is well informed on the current activities of the operating units under the boss's supervision, alerting him/her of any significant developments.
2 The private secretary keeps the boss informed of any informal news in the organization that may be of interest to him/her.

*Mail*
1 The private secretary receives all the boss's mail — both internal and external.
2 Where the private secretary feels that an item of the mail would be more appropriately dealt with by someone else she redirects it on her own initiative.
3 The private secretary decides whether to dispense completely with some items of the mail.
4 The private secretary scans the published material bringing to the boss's attention all items of importance which she knows are of special interest to him/her.
5 The private secretary drafts replies to routine letters.
6 The private secretary carefully studies each item of her boss's mail

and then attaches background notes to it from her file, where necessary, in order to facilitate action on it by her boss.

7 The private secretary decides whether the boss needs any additional information in order to take action on an item of the mail (i.e. outside of her file) and where possible obtains it for him/her.

8 When the private secretary finally takes the mail in to her boss, she ranks the various items in order of importance.

9 The private secretary researches and writes reports for her boss on special projects/issues which form part of her boss's responsibility.

10 The private secretary reminds her boss of the various deadlines on his/her reports and other written documents.

*Telephone*

1 The private secretary screens all the boss's incoming telephone calls.

2 The private secretary deals with routine calls herself.

3 Where the private secretary thinks that the telephone call can be handled elsewhere, she diplomatically refers the caller to someone else.

4 If the call is urgent the private secretary interrupts the boss's meeting in order for him/her to take it.

5 Where the boss is not available the private secretary tactfully enquires into the nature of the call and then passes on this message to her boss together with any other information she feels is necessary for action to be taken.

6 Where necessary the private secretary arranges for the boss to return the call at a set time.

7 All telephone calls to be made by the boss are grouped together with relevant information and files for ready reference.

8 The private secretary discusses with the boss all the telephone calls received in his/her absence and once decisions have been reached on them the private secretary returns the calls for her boss.

*Activities provided by the private secretary in the absence of her boss*

1 When the boss makes any business trips the private secretary arranges all the transport, hotel accommodation and his/her various appointments.

2 When the boss is away on a business trip the private secretary manages his/her work in his/her absence.

3 When the boss is away on a business trip the private secretary is required to take decisions that would not normally be handled by her if her boss was at the office.

4 When the boss is away the private secretary decides whether to hold certain items for his/her return, or whether to forward them to him/her.

5 Where the private secretary decides to forward certain information to the boss while he/she is away, she must assess the importance of it in terms of how quickly it ought to reach him/her (i.e. should she use the telephone, telex, registered mail or ordinary mail).

6 When the boss returns from a business trip the private secretary gives him/her all the backlog of correspondence and telephone messages in order of importance.

7 In the boss's absence the private secretary makes a special effort to keep in touch with company news on behalf of her boss.

## Perceptions of the 'ideal' private secretary

In this section the scores for the seven areas of communication activity in relation to the ideal private secretary are examined. These results are presented in Table 5.1. Three profiles are illustrated. One is the profile represented by the seven mean scores across all thirty secretaries for the seven areas of activity. In addition, similarly computed profiles are shown for the top five and bottom five private secretaries. Selection of the top and bottom five secretaries was made on the basis of total score achieved on the questionnaire (i.e. across all forty-eight statements). These two additional profiles were calculated in order to highlight the range of scores in each of the seven areas of activity.

Table 5.1 *Profiles of the 'ideal' private secretary by the sample over all by the top five private secretaries and by the bottom five private secretaries*

| Areas of communication activity (abbreviated) | Averages (means) | | |
|---|---|---|---|
| | Sample | Top 5 | Bottom 5 |
| Diary | 3.86 | 4 | 3.5 |
| Personal visitors | 3.67 | 3.97 | 3.1 |
| Mail | 3.65 | 3.94 | 3.1 |
| Support activities | 2.9 | 3.5 | 2.1 |
| Information source | 3.6 | 4 | 2.8 |
| Telephone | 3.8 | 3.97 | 3.5 |
| Boss absent | 3.7 | 3.91 | 3.37 |

Four points in Table 5.1 are immediately striking. First, all the averages are relatively high, that is, all are above the mid-point of the scale ( = 2). The area which consistently had the highest scores was the diary; in other words, the ideal private secretary participates most actively in tasks related to looking after the boss's diary. This includes knowing the location of the boss at all times, completely controlling his diary, ensuring that all appointments are kept, and making all the necessary administrative arrangements for visitors. Conversely, the area which consistently had the lowest scores was support activities. It would appear that only occasionally do top private secretaries expect to be engaged in support activities which cover planning the boss's work programmes, discussing work procedures, delegating and supervising work among the boss's subordinates, and acting as a surrogate for him at meetings. On examining the items contained under support activities it is not surprising that this area received the lowest scores, since it clearly consists of a set of relatively higher-order tasks. This is borne out by comparing the three profiles for the sample as a whole, the top five private secretaries and the bottom five private secretaries. In each case the profile assumed the same shape, in other words, secretaries score consistently lower on support activities than other activities, and consistently higher on tasks related to the diary and telephone.

In terms of examining the profiles for the top five and bottom five private secretaries, the largest deviations from the over-all average for both groups were the areas of support activities and informational activities. In relation to the bottom five secretaries, all of them never or rarely expected the private secretary to represent the boss at a meeting in his absence, and most of them felt that the secretary would rarely supervise a work programme for the boss or entertain guests on his behalf. In relation to the top five private secretaries, they all felt that it was general practice for a private secretary to be well informed on the current activities of the company, alerting the boss to any significant developments, and for the private secretary to ensure the boss knew of any informal news in the organization that might be of interest to him. 'Bosses rely on us for knowing what is going on.' In terms of support activities, all the private secretaries agreed that it was their duty to discuss work procedures generally with the boss and discuss improvements where necessary.

**Items receiving top and bottom scores**

In order to examine more closely the image of the ideal private secretary, the six statements (from the forty-eight) receiving the top and bottom scores across the thirty secretaries were identified. Those coming out on top (that is, most regularly occurring activities) were:

1 Always knows location of boss.
2 Receives all boss's mail.
3 Screens all boss's telephone calls.
4 Exercises discretion in making boss's appointments.
5 Handles telephone calls for boss and passes on relevant information.
6 When boss returns from a trip private secretary will give him all correspondence and messages ranked by her in order of importance.

It is interesting to note that the top three may be seen to be the basic demands of the secretarial role; if the secretary is seen as the boss's communication agent then it is critical that she knows the location of him and receives all his communications. Once the secretary has responsibility for these three areas then she begins to have the means to exert influence on the boss's communications. The latter three items receiving top scores relate to specific ways she handles appointments, telephone calls, and communications in general, when the boss is absent. These three items describe the relatively low-level ways in which the private secretary participates in her boss's communication system. There is one last point to be made in this section. It is easy to study the above six items and dismiss them as obvious aspects of a private secretary's role; they are, however, by no means characteristic of all private secretaries' jobs. One of the secretaries said that in her last job where she worked for one of the directors in a bank, the chairman regularly opened all the mail, not only for himself, but also for all his fellow directors!

Those statements making up the image of the ideal private secretary which scored lowest (that is, most rarely occurring activities) were as follows (working from the lowest up):

1 Entertains guests on behalf of boss.
2 Researches and writes reports which form part of the boss's responsibility.
3 Boss delegates supervision of work projects to the private secretary.
4 Private secretary represents boss at a meeting if he cannot attend.
5 When boss is absent private secretary is required to take decisions that she normally would not take.
6 Private secretary is used as a sounding-board for ideas.
7 Discusses work procedures with boss and suggests improvements.

The above items may be seen as the higher-order tasks of a private secretary; they are the more discretionary elements which a boss may allow his secretary to carry out for him. Evidence of all of these tasks emerged when interviewing the thirty private secretaries more closely about their own work. The top secretary in a large oil company regularly entertained guests on her boss's behalf; she recalled how she frequently had taken Ari Onassis to lunch, and had been involved in business negotiations with him. This particular private secretary knew her boss's clients extremely well, she had an expense account of her own, and on occasions like Christmas had the responsibility of deciding upon and purchasing expensive gifts for the major clients. Further to entertaining guests for the boss, this private secretary would also substitute for the chairman at certain internal meetings and company social functions. While she could not make top-level decisions completely on her own, she was given the opportunity to put forward both her own and her boss's point of view at such meetings and to report back to him on the proceedings. In other words, she was inextricably involved in all the issues dealt with by her boss. They would frequently discuss matters together and her views were listened to and often taken up. Her boss disliked all the external social functions attached to being a chairman of a large oil company, thus his secretary would often take his place on such occasions. Irrespective of her boss's presence she was always in attendance.

This particular private secretary also sometimes accompanied her boss to external meetings. She recalled how she had travelled to Egypt with her boss several times when he had negotiated with President Sadat. Her role there was to organize appointments for her boss from the hotel, and to take messages for him while he was at meetings. She also helped in arranging and attending any social functions involved in the visit. The presence of a woman in such a business situation was then (a number of years ago) extremely unusual, thus she gained a lot of attention from this activity. In general, however, she usually looked after the office in her boss's absence. During such times she was often required to take highly responsible decisions, which would only be taken by her boss in the normal course of events. She remembered how once her boss was called away overseas suddenly and so he asked her to do some share transactions. It consisted of investing £40,000 for him in shares; this entailed negotiating with a bank and deciding when was the best time to buy. This example is an interesting one because it not only highlights the responsibility and trust that the boss placed in his secretary, but it also stresses the importance of the secretary's authority by being recognized by outsiders — in this case, the bank.

Three points were frequently raised by the secretaries in relation to making decisions in the boss's absence. One is that the top man's office is a department of its own, basically consisting of the managing director and his secretary. Farther down the organization there is a bureaucratic structure which means that if a manager is away the decision gets neatly delegated to the relevant subordinate, according to the formal organization chart, or alternatively, it can get pushed up the hierarchy. At the top there is no automatic person to delegate a decision to, nor can it be pushed up, because by definition the top man is the decision ceiling of the organization. This means that it has to be the private secretary at that level who decides how to handle the decision; can it wait, should she make it, should it be delegated, and if so to whom? The second point about making decisions in the boss's absence is that they cannot usually be retracted. Normally, if the boss changes his mind on an issue the day afterwards, it can be retrieved, but if the secretary makes a decision and the boss doesn't return until five weeks afterwards it is usually too late to reverse it. There is thus an added weight of responsibility attached to making decisions in such circumstances. Finally, it is necessary to appreciate that the nature of decision-making at the top is rather different from that occurring at lower levels. At lower levels there are the everyday routine decisions but at the top, as one secretary said: 'There are no routine decisions, it's a case of trying to compare similar situations while assessing the uniqueness of each.' Thus the nature of decision-making at the top of organizations is such as to increase the private secretary's responsibility in the managing director's absence.

Regarding the remaining items which scored lowest on the image of the ideal private secretary, a number of the private secretaries in the study discussed work procedures with their bosses and, indeed, were used as sounding-boards for ideas. This applied not just to the boss but to the boss's subordinates, who used the private secretary as a barometer of the boss. One secretary described her office as the 'Citizens' Advice Bureau'. They knew that if she thought the ideas were worth mentioning to the boss that she would act as the effective 'go-between'.

'They plant the seeds with me and I water them,' said one secretary. The secretary is able to act as an effective barometer for the boss since she is the one who works closest to him, and therefore is likely to know more about his attitudes and values than anyone else. 'They not only consult me but are often guided by me, because they know I speak on behalf of the managing director.' She may not be used simply for evaluating and carrying ideas; it may be a case of deciding when is the best time, for example, for the marketing director to talk to the boss about his proposals. Timing the presentation of ideas can be crucial to their reception, and here the private secretary can be valuable in deciding when is the best time, since again she is more aware of his moods than anyone else.

Some of the top private secretaries actually research and write reports for their bosses. Reference has already been made to the secretary who regularly prepared situation reports for her boss, thus alerting him to the possibilities of any industrial problems that might emerge. Another secretary had the responsibility of preparing monthly progress reports for the board. This task clearly required the secretary to understand and analyse business situations, abstract the pertinent points, collate them, and present them in an interesting and logical form. In order to carry out this activity she had to keep herself constantly informed on the company's day-to-day performance.

### Relating the profile of the 'ideal' private secretary with the actual profile of top private secretaries

This profile of the 'ideal' private secretary was then compared to the actual profiles of the thirty private secretaries. The Spearman Rank correlation coefficient was computed; it was .64 (p<.01 level). In other words, there is a highly significant positive relationship between the way top private secretaries perceive the activities of the effective private secretary and the way they perceive their own activities. On account of this close similarity in profile, the results concerning the latter will not be discussed separately here.

### Conclusion

The results presented in this chapter should prompt all users of private secretaries to examine their own expectations of them. A useful exercise is for managers and their secretaries to respond jointly to the forty-eight statements on pp.80-3, relate the results with those emerging in this chapter, and then identify those areas in which the private secretaries could take on more responsibility.

# 6 | The Gatekeeper Position of the Top Private Secretary

In the last chapter attention was focused on how the thirty top private secretaries defined an effective private secretary, and how they perceived their own job activities. The amount of responsibility private secretaries saw themselves as having was examined in relation to seven key areas of their positions. In this chapter the influence exerted by top private secretaries is pursued in more depth; it involves an analysis of how the thirty top private secretaries actually behaved in their jobs. Three core areas of the boss's communication system were studied. They are how the private secretary handles the boss's personal visitors, mail, and telephone calls.

The objectives of this stage of the research were to measure three important dimensions of each of these areas of the private secretary's job:

1 The size of the communication system, that is, number of personal visitors, items of mail, telephone calls received on a daily basis.
2 The extent to which the private secretary has control over the communication system, that is, the percentage of visitors, mail, and telephone calls over which she controls the access to the managing director.
3 The means whereby the private secretary exerts her control over the communication system, that is, the precise ways in which she processes each piece of communication.

The first part of the chapter looks at how the private secretary controls the managing director's personal visitors, mail, and telephone calls. It endeavours to meet the three objectives set out above. The latter half of the chapter looks at the total amount of control and patterns of control exerted by the thirty top private secretaries.

### Control exercised by the private secretary over personal visitors

Figure 6.1 summarizes the main results obtained in this area. In general, secretaries arrange 91 per cent of their bosses' appointments. The remainder tend to be appointments arranged by the boss when he is away at a meeting requiring a follow-up. This element of the control process is absolutely complete; the boss relies totally on the private secretary; he does not expect her to consult with him on scheduling meetings at all. 'He's hopeless at making arrangements and also he hates to say "no"; of course, it is much easier to refuse when it comes from the secretary.' Not only does the secretary arrange the boss's diary but she also screens 85 per cent of his *ad hoc* intra-organizational callers during the day. On the whole this is relatively easy to carry out, since in the great majority of cases the secretary's office is situated between the boss's and the corridor, thus visitors must pass through it to reach the boss. The 15 per cent of callers who are automatically allowed access are the top directors: this might consist of the chairman and vice chairman. Altogether, the average number of *ad hoc* callers to the boss amounts to eighteen each day. This figure, on the surface, may not seem large, but it has to be remembered that other callers the secretary regularly deals with are the official ones with scheduled meetings, other directors and managers wishing to see the secretary specifically, and other secretaries, messengers, and chauffeurs. Thus a lot of the secretary's day is spent in handling visitors. One secretary said: 'I spend a lot of time just managing changeovers; if the boss isn't ready to see a visitor then I have to entertain him. This can take up to half an hour sometimes.'

Another secretary picked up this point. 'My office is like a waiting-room. The trouble is I can't get any work done while someone is here. ... Still, it's certainly a valuable way of keeping informed.' The information picked up by a secretary in this situation may be knowledge that is not divulged to the managing director; for example, reference may be made to a director who is about to retire. In such a case the secretary will alert her boss to the facts, and in the situation of a colleague-director retiring will arrange for a present to be sent to him. Often, however, the information picked up by a secretary from the boss's visitors is information which will also be divulged to the managing director. When this occurs it will alleviate the boss's need to communicate with his secretary on the proceedings of the meeting.

On the whole, secretaries try to encourage bosses to keep to their schedules: 'You have to, my boss spends about 75 per cent of his time in scheduled meetings and a further 15 per cent of his time in unscheduled meetings, so the demands made upon him are constant.'

The general principle applied in screening visitors to the boss is that executives from only one level below him are able to see him. Thus there is a strict bureaucratic system in operation whereby each subordinate works through his immediate manager. In some organizations where the managing director is considering an issue of very specialized interest he may see the person who has the greatest expertise in that area, in which case he may come from four or five levels down in the organization from the managing director. Another exception to this principle occurred in one organization where the managing director made a habit of meeting every recruit to management. Thus this involved the private secretary in liaising closely with the personnel director in keeping track of new recruits and arranging meetings with her boss. In general, managing directors of all the organizations studied spent a great proportion of their time in meetings with both internal and external executives. It is rare for them ever to be free for lunch. Where this did occur, private secretaries would usually anticipate this and set up internal lunches with the bosses' fellow directors.

In terms of gatekeeping visitors to the boss, private secretaries do not like to see themselves preventing access to him; instead, they see themselves controlling access to him in such a way as to maximize the boss's time. This they perceive as being of mutual benefit to both boss and personal visitors. It is interesting to note here that it is often the private secretary who has little chance of speaking to her boss during the day. Frequently she must wait until the very end of the day before having the opportunity to consult him about various issues, and this may mean staying until about 6.30 p.m.

In analysing how the private secretary handles *ad hoc* visitors to the boss (see Figure 6.1), the most striking statistic is that she effects 70 per cent of them in one way or another. The ways in which she effects them vary a great deal from one secretary to another. On average, however, the private secretary deals with 45 per cent of visitors' enquiries on her own, and automatically allows 30 per cent of visitors in to see the boss; she redirects 10 per cent to other executives, and in 15 per cent of cases the private secretary arranges for the caller to be contacted at a later date. Those who are allowed automatic access to the boss are usually the top directors who want 'five minutes' with him. Although five minutes often gets extended it is rare for it to go beyond twenty, simply because directors at that level respect one another's pressurized schedules. Occasionally, however, such a short *ad hoc* meeting will trigger off a series of meetings and action; for example, where news is given of a stoppage at a particular plant. Even

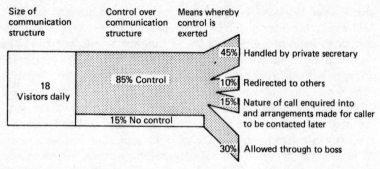

**Fig 6.1**  *An analysis of the top private secretary's control over the manager's personal visitors*

*This figure shows average (mean) number of* ad hoc *visitors wanting to see the managing director each day, the degree to which the private secretary controls their access to the managing director, and the means whereby she exerts her control over them.*

here, however, the managing director's role is only consultative; he does not usually participate in any negotiations. The situation is probably quite different in smaller companies where the managing director will be far more involved in the day-to-day running of the company's activities.

The private secretary deals with 45 per cent of the boss's visitors on her own. This may involve giving advice, answering queries, receiving information to be forwarded to the boss, or making decisions on his behalf. In some situations she redirects them to others. This may occur where a subordinate comes to her seeking advice from her boss, the latter is very busy, and she feels his query could be handled appropriately by another executive. The other 15 per cent of callers need to liaise with the boss but since he is unavailable the private secretary arranges for the boss to contact the caller. This may take place where the managing director needs to confirm a decision, sign a contract, or approve another director's action. Over all, the private secretary's role in gatekeeping personal visitors is one of protecting and buffering the boss. The secretary whose boss's name was George, was known as 'George's dragon', so effective was she at handling his visitors. In fact, this secretary saw as her great contribution: 'getting the boss to his appointments on time'.

Another secretary in evaluating her role said: 'I completely organize his day, deciding who will see him, when, and for how long.' The way the private secretary acts as an intermediary and 'pathsmoother' between her boss and his visitors also means that she maintains a great deal of contact with management and clerical staff throughout the head office. 'The private secretary is a potent force in establishing the popularity of a managing director. The private secretary represents the boss in her work, and to many who never actually meet the man, all their perceptions of him are gained from the private secretary.' This refers to the private secretary's role both in her boss's personal communication network and in her own personal communication network.

## Control exercised by the private secretary over mail

The private secretary's role in her boss's communication structure, defined by the flow of mail, is shown in Figure 6.2.

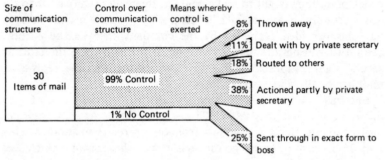

**Fig 6.2** *An analysis of the top private secretary's control over the manager's mail*

*This figure shows the average (mean) number of items sent daily in the mail to the managing director, the degree to which the private secretary controls their access to the managing director, and the means whereby she exerts her control over them.*

The most striking feature of Figure 6.2 is the high control the private secretary has over her boss's mail. The average amount of control was 99 per cent; in other words, there is virtually total control in this area of the boss's communication system. While there was a uniform response in terms of degree of control, there was a varied response with regard to the size of this particular control system. Between twelve and seventy-five was the mean number of items received each day in the post. This averages out across secretaries at thirty items a day. Bearing in mind that these organizations were selected along common structural dimensions, it is fascinating to speculate as to why this range is so enormous. Is it that the managing director encourages a certain style of communicating which determines the degree of written versus other forms of communicating? The point here, is that where the boss does support written communication, then the secretary naturally has much more opportunity to operate her gatekeeper power. This point becomes particularly significant in the light of Mintzberg's finding that top executives tend to gravitate away from written communications in favour of verbal ones.[1] This element of the boss's communication structure is important for another reason. When personally visiting the boss or telephoning him, the caller can calculate how much information to give the private secretary; in the case of writing to him, this option is not open. As a result, the private secretary gains a lot of information from managing this aspect of the boss's communications.

There are two reasons why the managing director, in particular, receives such a heavy delivery of mail. The first is because if outsiders wishing to communicate with the organization are unsure at which point they ought to make contact, they will usually write to the top. Secondly, if an outsider is attempting to make a complaint or have his/her idea evaluated by the company then he/she is more certain of getting attention by writing to the managing director. In several organizations managing directors will, on principle, reply to all mail personally addressed to them.

In terms of how private secretaries react to the boss's mail, Figure 6.2 indicates that they affect 75 per cent of it. As with personal visitors, these effects vary greatly from one secretary to another. Thus only 25 per cent of letters go through in the exact form in which they were received by the private secretary; thirty-eight per cent of the boss's mail is actioned partly by the private secretary. This may include looking out past correspondence, gathering information in order to process the letter (either from within òr outside the company), and drafting a reply to it. 'I try to anticipate my boss's information needs. In this way I can get as much of the answer together as possible.'

A further 18 per cent of mail gets re-routed to other executives: 'So many people write to the managing director because he's the top man, so a lot can be automatically delegated to others.' 'A letter shouldn't get to the boss unless there's a background to it.'

This latter quote is interesting. It suggests that nothing is initiated at the top. In fact, this observation accords with others made by top secretaries. 'The managing director does not make decisions, he only refers, modifies, rejects, or confirms decisions made by others.'

Eighteen per cent of mail is re-routed by the private secretary to other executives. The responsibility of the private secretary here is in deciding who should do what. This decision is based on her perception of what her boss would do in the situation. A number of private secretaries, when interviewed, stressed the importance of knowing the appropriate person to whom to delegate matters. This refers to the boss's style of managing and it is something that the private secretary gradually learns over time. In general, when mail is re-routed, three courses of action may be taken. The private secretary may decide to redirect certain pieces of mail to other executives; in other words, she completely transfers responsibility for them. Alternatively, she may re-route mail but follow up the decision made upon it. In this situation she retains the opportunity of further effecting the information, since in the final stage she will be consulted on the action taken. A good example of how this option was implemented was where the boss was requested to give his advice on a specialized subject. This letter was forwarded by the private secretary to the person in the company most qualified to deal with the subject. He sketched a reply and sent it back to the managing director's secretary who then translated the letter into 'the boss's language'. It was then read by the managing director before being sent out.

The third option open to the private secretary in delegating mail is for her boss to see a copy of the redirected letter as well as a copy of the reply. In this situation the private secretary and her boss have the ultimate decision on the actioning of the letter. This alternative allows the existence of a 'safety net'; if the managing director wants to handle a letter that his secretary has delegated, he has a means of retrieving it. This latter option is likely to occur where complaints are received. 'These are fragile items of mail requiring great care.'

In fact, here the private secretary may make a few preliminary enquiries before deciding to delegate the complaint to the appropriate divisional director. When the reply is finally sent out it may be modified by the managing director (and/or his private secretary) and signed by him. In exceptional cases where the complaint is sufficiently serious to warrant it, the final letter may be written by the managing director.

Eleven per cent of the correspondence is processed totally by the private secretary. This may include several types of mail. It will certainly consist of all letters arranging meetings with the boss, whether they be to set up meetings, confirm them, or cancel them. They will usually all include letters relating to decisions made about social functions, contributions to charity organizations, retirement dinners, annual sales conferences, and visitors coming to stay in the company flat. Where the private secretary replies to letters she may sign them in her name, and not in her boss's. Most secretaries, however, said: 'It is important they're signed by him and not by me — it's a mark of respect.'

This again underlines the 'backstage' role of the secretary. She is prepared to deny her own existence in order to build up her boss's reputation. Handling the mail can be very time-consuming; for instance, arranging a dinner involves getting specifications and quotes from different hotels, having meetings with hotel managers, choosing menus, making up invitations, and designing table arrangements, etc. Such social functions and meetings may or may not be allied to the organization. All the managing directors studied have extra-organizational positions, in some cases six or more; these include sitting on government bodies, school councils, industrial committees, and boards of other companies. A number of private secretaries said that it can take nearly a day just to arrange one meeting allied to one of these activities. This is not surprising because the private secretary is co-ordinating a group of top people in industry, all of whom have constant demands being made upon them.

The other major component of this category of mail is the general information which flows into the managing director's office: management journals, trade journals, house journals, government reports, minutes from meetings, intra-organizational project reports, project proposals, and details of work assignments carried out. All get sent to the managing director. It is the private secretary's job to scan through them, abstracting or passing on in complete form any information she thinks will be valuable to him, or that he would like to see. This is an enormous task; organizations generate a lot of paper and the managing director's office is seen as the focus for it. 'This office is seen far more as a place for receiving information than for sending it out. Having said that, if anyone is looking for information in the company, he'll telephone me, because if it's in the building it will be here.'

Finally, 8 per cent of mail, after being sorted, gets thrown away by the private secretary. This happens where she is confident that neither her boss nor any other director would want such information. This category of mail generally consists of journals, details of management courses and new management books, soliciting of business from estate agents, insurance companies, etc. It is in this situation, that secretaries who have worked in the organizations for many years are likely to be best able to deal with this mail.

There is one last point to raise in relation to the private secretary's gatekeeping of mail. She not only screens letters coming in for the boss, but a number of secretaries also screen those written by the boss before they are sent out. 'I never send letters out that I don't approve of,' said one forthcoming secretary. She recalled a number of arguments she had had with her boss over how he had composed a letter. This illustrates how the private secretary may gatekeep not only incoming mail, but also outgoing mail.

## Control exercised by the private secretary over telephone calls

The profile that emerges in this sphere of the boss's communication structure reinforces those emerging from the two previous areas. On average, top private secretaries screen 97 per cent of their bosses' telephone calls. Thus it is apparent that the gatekeeper role of the top private secretaries is exerted almost to its maximum capacity in all parts of the bosses' communication systems. 'I must protect my boss as much as possible.' 'I try to keep as many calls away from him as I can.'

One of the main reasons for screening telephone calls is that top bosses spend nearly all day in meetings and it is extremely disruptive to receive calls in these circumstances. 'He hates to be interrupted ... and never takes a raw call.' 'I discretely keep away calls that can be dealt with by others, or by him later on.'

In general, the bosses in the sample wanted their secretaries to filter all their telephone calls. In only two cases did the secretaries filter only the external calls. This was done in the belief that intra-organizational members are responsible enough not to contact the managing director unless really necessary.

The actual number of telephone calls received each day varied from ten to sixty-three, thus the average figure masks the tremendous differences between secretaries. Secretaries were also quick to point out that numbers of telephone calls, like pieces of mail and numbers of personal visitors, vary very much from one day to the next. Interestingly, however, the private secretary who reported having the largest number of telephone calls each day (sixty-five) also had the most visitors (thirty). She did not receive the most mail, but this is probably accounted for by the fact that this was the only office in which the managing director had a male personal assistant. This meant that mail went first to the personal assistant's secretary, then to him, and then came to the private secretary. She had, on average, twelve pieces of mail each day.

In terms of the way top private secretaries deal with telephone calls, the most striking statistic from Figure 6.3 is that 44 per cent are handled completely by them. This contrasts with the comparable figure for mail of 11 per cent, but is similar to the comparable figure for personal visitors, 45 per cent. It is apparent from interviewing the

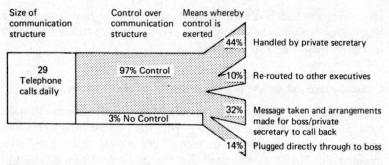

**Fig. 6.3**  *An analysis of the top private secretary's control over the manager's telephone calls.*

*This figure shows the average (mean) number of telephone calls made to the managing director each day, the degree to which the private secretary controls their access to the managing director, and the means whereby she exerts her control over them.*

secretaries that a large number of these telephone calls are concerned with setting up internal meetings. It must be recalled here that it is not unusual for a managing director to spend 80 per cent of his day at meetings, thus it is not surprising that much of his secretary's time is consumed in arranging and co-ordinating his movements. Other calls the secretary handles herself are those allied to social functions she is responsible for, queries and advice from other directors and secretaries, and a large number of calls which involve the receipt of information which may be of interest to the managing director.

Taking messages and arranging for either the boss or herself to call back can save an enormous amount of time for the former. First, it means that he is not disrupted from his activities to answer the call. Secondly, it means that if any background letters or information need to be gathered before the call can be answered, then the secretary can do all this for the boss. Lastly, it means that the boss allocates his time to top priority tasks first, since when the secretary passes on telephone messages to him, she sorts them in order of importance. Those he considers less pressing he may ask the secretary to deal with, after discussing the nature of the replies with her. The major benefit of having a 'gatekeeper' private secretary, then, is that the boss can allocate his time to the maximum advantage. 'I take away all the details,' summed up one secretary when evaluating her role.

An alternative option open to the private secretary, in saving her boss's time where telephone calls are concerned, is to re-route them to other executives. This is done on average 10 per cent of the time, thus it is a less popular option. The top private secretaries said that they frequently receive calls from the Press; all these, on principle, are transferred to public relations. If the managing director is unlikely to be able to return an important call for a day or two because of pressing commitments, then again the secretary may decide to transfer it to the next in command. In general, there appeared to be a very bureaucratic system operating in each of the organizations studied, such that contact upwards must be made via the immediate link above. Thus the private secretary, with a few exceptions, makes and maintains contact primarily with the board of directors. Contacts emanating from any level below the latter will generally be referred to the appropriate point at board level. This system helps to avoid the situation of the man at the top getting inundated with communications. Even then, one of the secretaries said: 'You constantly have too much to do, so you must be able to carry out your job without panicking.'

Fourteen per cent of telephone calls are plugged straight through to the managing director. This is likely to occur if he is not engaged in an important meeting, if the caller is also an extremely busy person, or if the piece of information is 'red-hot news'. The importance of the private secretary in this situation may be in locating the boss and getting the call transferred. This is one of the reasons why it is critical for the secretary always to know the whereabouts of the boss. As is evident, this situation is relatively usual, thus supporting the picture of the active role played by the top private secretary in the boss's telephone component of his communications structure.

### Developing an index of the influence wielded by the top private secretaries in their bosses' communication systems

The results discussed in this chapter and summarized in Figures 6.1, 6.2, and 6.3, formed the basis of the development of a total index of the influence wielded by individual top private secretaries in the three areas of their bosses' communications. The intuitive idea behind the index was that the various ways a private secretary processes an item of mail, a personal visitor, or a telephone call may be defined in terms of 'degrees of effect' on the communication. In other words, answering a letter herself is not equivalent in influence/effect to passing on the letter to the boss for him to reply to. With this in mind, the three sets of actions relating to how a top private secretary deals with personal visitors, mail, and telephone calls were assessed in terms of how much influence the private secretary was seen to exert in each situation. The three sets of actions were treated separately. This assessment took place by showing the three sets of actions to a panel of outside 'experts', who had had considerable experience working with secretaries. They were asked to rank the actions in order of importance, defined in terms of the effect the private secretary has on the communication. They then repeated this procedure for each of the other two sets of actions.

The results were as follows. In terms of handling personal visitors, the greatest weight was given to those private secretaries who deal with visitors on their own. The next heaviest weight was allocated to 'redirecting visitors to other executives', on the basis that this completely eliminated the communicational input to the boss, but it was not the private secretary who actually processed it fully. Of less importance was taking a message and arranging for boss or private secretary to contact the caller; this was because in this situation the boss was given the option of receiving and processing the piece of communication. The secretary was seen to have least effect where she allowed the visitor to see the boss straightaway. The weights were thus allocated as follows:

1　Handle on her own.      4
2　Redirect to others.      3
3　Enquire into nature of call
　　and arrange for boss/private
　　secretary to contact caller.      2
4　Allow straight through to
　　see boss.      1

Where a private secretary either handled the item of mail on her own or threw it away, this was considered to be the situation in which she exerted most influence. In both of these instances the communication did not go through to the boss. The action of next importance was redirecting mail to other executives, because again this prevented the communicational input from reaching the boss. (Of course, he may see it at a later date if the executive to whom it has been forwarded refers it to the managing director.) Of less significance, but a situation in which the secretary is still seen to exert influence, is where she partly actions the item; of least importance is the situation where the private secretary passes through the letter intact to the managing director. The weights were thus allocated as follows:

1　Item is thrown away.      4
2　Item is dealt with by private
　　secretary.      4
3　Item is redirected.      3

4 Item is partly actioned.          2
5 Item is sent through to boss.     1

Telephone calls were assessed in a similar way. Where the private secretary handled it herself was considered to be the situation in which she exerted most influence; where she redirected it, it was considered to be less important. Least important of all was where she transferred the call straight to the boss and of more importance (but of less significance than redirecting it) was where she took a message and arranged for the boss or herself to call back. The weights in this area were thus allocated as follows:

1 Handled by private secretary.    4
2 Re-routed.                       3
3 Take message and arrange for
  caller to be contacted.          2
4 Plug call straight through to
  boss.                            1

It is worth noting that the panel did not find it easy to reach decisions on the ranking of the various actions, albeit that the final weights reflected majority decisions. The difficulties stemmed mainly from the fact that all communications are not of equal importance. Thus it is difficult to evaluate whether answering a somewhat routine letter is more important than partly actioning a letter requiring a top-level policy decision. The criterion used, however, was the degree of influence applied to the communication by virtue of the existence of the private secretary. All communications, then, were regarded as equal. This does place slightly artificial parameters around the final index. This problem suggests that in any further research on the subject, some kind of weighting system needs to be applied in order to reflect the differing amounts of importance attached to the various communications.

The indices were then computed by multiplying the percentage of actions falling into any one classification of action by the weight allocated to that category, and then adding together the scores from each category.

It was possible for each index to range from 100 to 400. The indices for all individuals for each of the three areas of communications are shown in Table 6.1. Alongside the indices are the rankings of the secretaries in the three areas. The average (mean) index for each area is also computed across the secretaries. It is interesting to observe that the average (mean) index of influence exerted over personal visitors is

Table 6.1   *Indices of influence together with ranking of individuals on the basis of the indices*

N = 27

| Individual | Telephone calls | | Personal visitors | | Mail | |
|---|---|---|---|---|---|---|
| 100 | 315 | 8th | 154 | 25th | 280 | 5th |
| 101 | 290 | 11th | 310 | 6th | 280 | 5th |
| 102 | 250 | 19th | 325 | 5th | 265 | 9th |
| 103 | 369 | 1st | 327 | 4th | 330 | 1st |
| 104 | 366 | 2nd | 338 | 3rd | 275 | 7th |
| 105 | 227 | 22nd | 297 | 8th | 285 | 4th |
| 107 | 283 | 14th | 234 | 15th | 184 | 24th |
| 108 | 240 | 20th | 305 | 7th | 240 | 14th |
| 109 | 330 | 5th | 289 | 9th | 245 | 13th |
| 110 | 272 | 16th | 157 | 23rd | 208 | 23rd |
| 111 | 265 | 17th | 216 | 18th | 310 | 2nd |
| 112 | 300 | 9th | – | | 250 | 12th |
| 114 | 265 | 17th | 265 | 11th | 211 | 21st |
| 115 | 280 | 15th | 142 | 25th | 210 | 22nd |
| 116 | 158 | 26th | 104 | 26th | 152 | 25th |
| 117 | 233 | 21st | 212 | 19th | 221 | 17th |
| 119 | 335 | 4th | 202 | 20th | 270 | 8th |
| 120 | 329 | 6th | 345 | 2nd | 220 | 18th |
| 121 | 290 | 11th | 198 | 22nd | 225 | 16th |
| 122 | 325 | 7th | 198 | 22nd | 265 | 9th |
| 123 | 215 | 25th | 252 | 12th | 139 | 26th |
| 124 | 285 | 13th | 250 | 13th | 219 | 19th |
| 125 | 295 | 10th | 225 | 16th | 215 | 20th |
| 126 | 220 | 23rd | 225 | 16th | 262 | 11th |
| 127 | 216 | 24th | 283 | 10th | 290 | 3rd |
| 128 | 108 | 27th | 244 | 14th | 231 | 15th |
| 129 | 342 | 3rd | 351 | 1st | 129 | 27th |
| | X = 274 | | X = 230 | | X = 237 | |

similar to that over mail: 230 compared to 237. The average (mean) index of influence exerted over telephone calls is not significantly different — 274. The reason for it being larger is a result of the fact that most secretaries reported handling many telephone calls on their own (44 per cent was the average number across the secretaries). Although the amount of influence exerted in each category of the communication system was similar when aggregated across secretaries, it was not similar when broken down by individual secretary. The three indices and the three rankings made on the basis of the indices were quite different for the majority of secretaries. The most consistent sets of rankings were held by secretary 116 (26th, 26th, 25th) and secretary 103 (1st, 4th, 1st), and the most inconsistent sets of rankings were held by secretary 127 (24th, 10th, 3rd) and secretary 129 (3rd, 1st, 27th). The most notable characteristic of Table 6.1, then, is the inconsistency in the indices and rankings for each secretary. This indicates that the amount of influence a secretary exerts varies considerably across the different communication systems. The differences in amount of influence exercised both between secretaries and across communication systems are probably explained by the disparities in working styles of the respective bosses. As one secretary summed up, 'You must work according to the way he [the boss] works. In general it's no good trying to fight his working rhythm; unless you can fit it you'd better leave.'

## Allocating priorities to information

Traditionally, the power or influence of the organizational gate-keeper is defined in terms of the way he/she *changes* the information; thus concepts such as omission, distortion, exaggeration, and condensation are applied. However, the gatekeeper not only effects the actual shape of the communication but also the timing of its arrival. This in turn constitutes an important factor in examining the attitude to it of the communicatee. Strangely enough, while this has been long recognized in the theory of attitude change, it has not before been analysed in relation to the theory of organizational gatekeepers.

In order to examine whether secretaries do distinguish between items of information in terms of allocating priorities to processing them, at the conclusion of the study the private secretaries were asked to state the order in which they would deal with an in-tray of items. The latter consisted of a typical cross-section of items in a secretary's in-tray, ranging from diary appointments to incoming mail and telephone calls, some being very urgent, others less so. If the secretaries did not respond to the items in the order they were in their in-trays, then this constituted another means of exercising their influence upon them. The results of this exercise may be summarized as follows:

1 In no case was there a unanimous decision by the secretaries to treat the item in the order it arrived.
2 Only in the case of five items did the largest percentage of secretaries agree with its actual ordering in the in-tray.
3 In all but one item there was a wide range of priorities allocated.

In conclusion, then, secretaries differ greatly in the way they allocate priorities to their bosses' communications. This may partly explain the variance in the ways the secretaries actually processed the different communications, as described earlier in this chapter.

# 7 | Conclusions

In this brief concluding chapter the main results of my research study are presented, along with my interpretations of them; finally, their implications are discussed..

At a general level it is evident that many organizations give little or no attention to analysing their real secretarial needs (that is, on the basis of managerial work-load, as opposed to managerial status), and considering how these are best satisfied. The lack of any strategic plans and standard personnel policies, together with a noticeable absence of any management training on using secretaries, help to precipitate a situation in which secretaries are under-utilized and treated in an arbitrary, and occasionally demeaning, way. As a result, organizations suffer from excessive secretarial costs, low productivity, and high labour turnover; managers suffer from their secretaries' lack of interest in the work and lack of commitment to their bosses; and secretaries suffer from low job satisfaction and the absence of any planned career development.

Looking more closely at the actual nature of secretarial activities, it is apparent that as secretaries move up the hierarchy they tend to undertake significantly more administrative tasks than mechanistic ones. The extent to which secretaries carry out administrative duties, however, could be greatly increased if managers were more willing to delegate to their secretaries. It is probably no coincidence that it was found that as secretaries became more self-initiating in their work activities so they tended to become more efficient in terms of time lost 'waiting for work'. In addition, as secretaries become more self-initiating in their work activities so they also tended to be more internally motivated and satisfied with their jobs. A crucial spin-off for managers is that they are relieved of some of their low-level tasks and so in turn can also be more productive.

At the top of organizations, where secretaries traditionally operate in the one-to-one working relationship with their managers, secretaries carry out a variety of administrative tasks. These tasks all tend to stem from the secretary's gatekeeper position in her boss's communication network. Theoretically, this position gives the secretary almost complete control over the boss's communications. It also means that she has the opportunity to wield a great deal of influence. The extent to which she can influence matters, while primarily connected to the gatekeeper position she occupies, is also related to her personality and the number of years she has worked in the organization. The last point is important and frequently underestimated. Many top secretaries have well-developed personal contacts throughout the organization and have an extensive knowledge of the organization's activities — and sometimes even its secrets.

The amount of influence wielded by top secretaries in their gatekeeper positions is considerable. In my study it was shown that they had 85 per cent control over their bosses' visitors, 97 per cent control over their telephone calls, and 99 per cent control over their mail (see Figure 7.1). Interestingly, there were no significant relationships

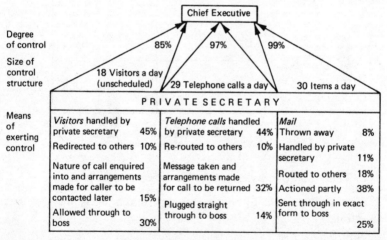

**Fig 7.1** *An empirical analysis of the top private secretary's gatekeeper position in the managing director's communication structure*

between the amounts of influence wielded in each of the three communication systems. This finding was also forcibly borne out in Chapter 3, where five private secretaries in different kinds of jobs were studied. These five secretaries differed quite markedly in terms of their perceptions of their primary roles, varying from allocator of the boss's time to filterer of the boss's information. This prompts the question of secretarial styles of working. Over the past twenty or thirty years a great deal of time and effort has been channelled into developing appropriate instruments for diagnosing managerial styles, and of confronting managers with their profiles as an aid to improving performance.

Perhaps now is the time to think of developing the concept of secretarial styles. In my own research it became increasingly evident to me that secretaries varied considerably in terms of how they dealt with their bosses' communications, particularly so in the bosses' absence. The two main dimensions along which secretaries differed were:

1 The degree to which the secretary herself makes decisions and takes action.
2 The degree to which the secretary involves others (i.e. apart from her boss) in making decisions and taking action.

Table 7.1    *Developing a typology of secretarial styles*

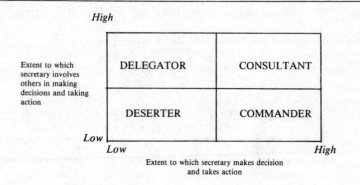

In Table 7.1 four styles can be identified and defined:

1 *Low* on the extent to which secretary makes decisions and takes action.
and
*Low* on the extent to which secretary involves others in making decisions and taking action.

This is the *deserter* style of managing. This type of secretary neither makes a decision herself nor allows others to make it for her. Her strategy is to 'shelve' decisions until the boss is in a position to make them himself. This style is exemplified by the secretary who acknowledges her boss's letters but leaves to him all the action to be taken on them.

2 *Low* on the extent to which secretary makes decisions and takes action.

and

*High* on the extent to which secretary involves others in making decisions and taking action.

This is the *delegator* style of managing. This type of secretary recognizes that decisions should be made quickly and delegates them to other executives. The reasons for delegating decisions to others may be that she does not want the responsibility for making the decision, she feels that other executives will make 'better' decisions, or she may feel that the decision is more appropriately handled by another executive. The responsibility of this type of secretary is to decide to whom to delegate the decision.

3 *High* on the extent to which secretary makes decisions and takes action.

and

*Low* on the extent to which secretary involves others in making decisions and taking action.

This is the *commander* style of managing. This secretary recognizes that decisions must be made quickly and feels that it is 'right' for her to make them. She turns to nobody for advice. This secretary may be seen to exert the most influence since decisions are kept entirely within her domain. This style is best exemplified by the secretary who attends meetings on behalf of her boss.

4 *High* on the extent to which the secretary makes decisions and takes action.

and

*High* on the extent to which secretary involves others in making decisions and taking action.

This is the *consultant* style of managing. This type of secretary recognizes that decisions should be made quickly and feels that other executives can valuably contribute to the decision-making situation. Thus this type of secretary does not relinquish responsibility for the decision, like the delegator, but does consult other directors and executives in order to elicit advice or information. This style is exemplified by the secretary who sets up a retirement dinner in terms of choosing a hotel and menu in consultation with the personnel manager, who arranges the Press release with Public Relations, and when everything is tentatively decided sends memoranda to everyone involved to keep them informed as to what has happened.

Shifting from the main results of my research and my interpretations of them to the implications for organizations, I think four are worth highlighting. First, I think many managers (and possibly secretaries also) are unaware of their secretaries' potential, so it is hoped that this book may help to open their eyes as to how to develop this potential. This will become all the more important when word processing has taken over the traditional mechanistic tasks associated with secretaries. Secondly, following on from that point, once new opportunities have been recognized whereby secretaries can operate more effectively (and more happily), then individual managers and secretaries need to work closely together to ensure they synchronize working styles. This means that the secretary should be aiming to complement her boss, rather than supplement or substitute for him. Training can play an important role here in developing such teamwork.

Thirdly, this book raises the issue as to how organizations use the secretarial role. The irrational bases of the role have been highlighted. At the top of organizations this is particularly true where secretaries, for example, may become 'redundant' when their bosses retire. Much more attention needs to be focused on strategically planning for secretaries and developing personnel policies in relation to them.

Lastly, this research prompts the issue of sex roles in organizations. As more women rise in the managerial hierarchy it is interesting to speculate as to whether the boss-secretary relationship on a female/female or female/male situation is the same as a male/female one. Discussions with a number of managers suggest that it is the female/female one that is likely to be the most problematic; perhaps this is because there is a sexual identification, which in turn poses threats to the relationship. The whole subject of the roles of the sexes needs to be surfaced and exposed in the light of the recent legislation and changing attitudes towards women in organizations.

These four implications, stemming directly from my own study of secretaries, are sufficient arguments for reappraising the role of secretaries. When consideration is given, however, to the radical repercussions of the introduction of word processing systems, then it is indeed timely to shake up the secretarial world.

# *Appendix*
# Research
# Methodology

The purpose of this appendix is to outline the approach I adopted in carrying out the research study, which provided the basic material for this book. The actual methods applied in any piece of research fundamentally determine the type of results that will be derived from it. Depending on the nature of the study so certain data gathering methods will be more appropriate than others. However, in the end, no one method is going to offer all the characteristics needed in order to produce the desired data base. Triangulation or the use of multiple methods overcomes the biases stemming from limiting oneself to only one method of data gathering.[1] It has constituted the basis for this particular piece of research. I have attempted to relate the methodology applied to the particular problems emerging at each stage of the study, and also to relate the methods among themselves in order to optimize the validity of the ultimate findings.

## First stage

Although the stated aim of the research was to develop and subsequently test a model of how the managing director's private secretary acts as a gatekeeper in her boss's communication system, this, in fact, did not evolve until a fairly late stage in the research process. I began by being interested in exploring the function of secretaries in organizations since my own experience suggested that they clearly affected management performance, and yet they have been largely ignored in any theoretical treatment of the subject. My initial concern, then, was to observe how a complete system of secretaries operates in an organization, in terms of studying secretaries' activities and analysing their attitudes towards their jobs. I felt that such a picture would give me some kind of broad framework into which I could then go on to delimit the precise parameters of a suitable scientific study.

The opportunity to carry out such a project came when I was asked to participate, as a member of a consultancy team, on a job evaluation and job satisfaction study on all the secretaries in a large professional service organization in London. The study, as it was initially conceived by management, aimed at measuring secretarial productivity by means of an organization and methods analysis. Apparently management experienced problems with their secretaries in terms of there being a high turnover, and there was felt to be low productivity. It was hoped that the study would identify areas of inefficiency which could then subsequently be tackled by changes in the organization of secretarial services.

I regarded this way of approaching the problem as very limiting, hence I suggested that this hard activity analysis needed to be supplemented by an attitudinal survey that would attempt to ascertain the secretaries' own feelings towards their jobs, as well as giving them the opportunity of suggesting how they could be more efficiently used by management. The rationale behind this proposal was that it was only by trying to analyse the jobs from the secretaries' viewpoints that one could begin to understand their orientations to their jobs and explain their work behaviour.

Management accepted the proposed idea of incorporating discussions with the secretaries, thus the ultimate structure of the data collection stage of the study was as follows:

1 Internal statistics on number and distribution of secretaries across departments; figures for labour turnover; and salary structure.
2 Information from the managers/bosses with regard to their secretarial needs and their evaluations of their current secretaries.
3 Diary sheets filled in by secretaries on a daily basis over a two-week period, during which time information on the number and the nature of tasks undertaken was recorded.
4 Group discussions (each containing approximately eight) with all but the top six secretaries, in which an attempt was made to obtain reactions to their jobs, together with their recommendations on how they might be more efficiently used, and on how their jobs could be made more satisfying.
5 At the very top level in the company interviews were held individually with the six secretaries concerned.

The data collection period extended over a period of three weeks, the group discussions and activity analyses being carried out simultaneously. The study was, by design, extremely wide ranging, with data being collected from a number of different sources and from a variety of perspectives. It thus provided me with a rich source of material with which to familiarize myself with the nature of secretarial work and the orientations of secretaries towards their jobs. This data forms the basis of the case study reported in Chapter 2.

## Second stage

As a result of completing the case study, I developed, *inter alia*, an understanding of how the secretary's role differentiates itself up the hierarchy: ranging broadly from the situation of working in a pool to working for a group of managers; to that of working for two managers; to working exclusively for an individual manager. One of the key characteristics of this model is the nature of the dependency relationship existing between the boss and secretary. This ties in with the comments made in Chapter 1 on the progression of secretaries up the organizational hierarchy.

It was observed that increasing personalization of the boss-secretary relationship and increasing control over the boss's communication system typified the upward movement. The shift from secretary dependent on boss to boss dependent on secretary is the structural result of these two changes in relationship. Clearly, at the bottom of the hierarchy the secretary (or more precisely the shorthand typist) is totally dependent on her boss for her work activities; but as secretaries ascend the organization, that dependency tends to change, until at the very top the boss can be seen to be the dependent one. At this level the boss expects the secretary to take the initiative and to develop his activities for him, rather than him issuing her with directives. It is this dependency and inherent in it, the discretionary element of the top secretary's job, that intrigued me. By virtue of the fact that bosses depended upon the secretaries in, what might be broadly defined as, their communication systems, so the secretaries acquired access to a source of power. At this stage, then, I was keen to go on to develop an understanding of the secretary's role in her parallel boss's communication system. This stage of the research process, then, reflected a concern for identifying the types of roles played by the private secretary in managing the boss's communications. The focus of the enquiry had thus shifted from secretaries *in toto* to secretaries who were attached to individual bosses.

In order to carry out this stage of the research I gained access to two organizations — one educational establishment and one large industrial company in London — where I studied five private secretaries.

The latter were all 'attached' to the chairman, deputy chairman, managing director, or director of their respective organizations. I thus concentrated my attention on those private secretarial positions allied to the top (in terms of the formal hierarchical charting of the organizations concerned) of the structures. This is in accordance with the belief that the nearer one gets to the organizational centre of control and decision-making, the more pronounced is the emphasis on information exchange.

The purposes of this stage of the fieldwork were threefold:

1 To gain an initial understanding of how managers (defined as chairman, deputy chairman, director) used their private secretaries in the management of their incoming communication. (At this stage a 'private secretary' was defined as any permanent employee recruited as a 'private secretary' by the company.)

2 To consider whether there was any variance in the informational activities carried out by these private secretaries, and if so, to what extent this could be attributed to the differing needs of the managerial positions to which they were allied.

3 To develop a set of variables that could be used in the structured observational part (third stage) of the fieldwork, where the communicational activities of a number of private secretaries would be analysed. This included a detailed mapping of the communications processed by each private secretary during a working day.

While some time was spent with individual bosses, the main focus of the research was on the selected sample of private secretaries.

The role of the participant observer may take many forms according to the mix of observation and interviewing employed. In this case I entered the organizations as an 'observer participant'. That is to say, I made public to both chairman/director and his private secretary, in each case, that I was keen to obtain an understanding of the part played by the private secretary within the organization's structure. I was intentionally vague in my briefing in order that I might not restrict myself to the information that I would be given access to — assuming such a role gives the social scientist the maximum freedom in gathering information, but at the price of accepting maximum constraints in interpreting the data.[2] There are two other problems to this approach. The researcher may impart his own assumptions, concepts, and theories into the behaviour of the participants. Lastly, the nature of the method precludes the use of a large sample, thereby making generalizations from the data difficult to assert.[3]

These being the accompanying disadvantages to participant

observation, I make no claims to either generating or testing a set of hypotheses from this element of the fieldwork, *per se*. Instead, I used this methodology in the context of two organizations for the purposes of obtaining an in-depth understanding of how a small number of private secretaries function in relation to their bosses' communication systems.

The attraction of using participant observation, however, is that it allows the researcher to observe and question intensively where necessary, and, at the same time, be systematic. It also allows the researcher to obtain far more 'powerful' data on activity content than any comparative diary study would do. At the same time, the method incorporates a control on biases, selective perception, and interpretation of the data. It thus offers some form of 'objective standards' against which to check the measurements.

One overriding advantage of participant observation compared to, for example, the 'diary' approach, is that while it gives the researcher a certain degree of discipline in obtaining certain types of structured data, it simultaneously offers flexibility in gaining supplementary data by open-ended observation. That is to say, the researcher is able to elaborate upon the 'basic structured data' with other detailed information plus other anecdotal material, where this seems important to an understanding of the situation.

In conclusion, this second stage of the research fieldwork, the findings of which are discussed in Chapter 3, aimed to focus on a fairly systematic and in-depth study of the communication activities of a small number of private secretaries.

## Third stage

The aim of the third and last stage of the research was to test, in a systematic and precise way, the gatekeeper role of the private secretary in the managing director's communication system. The thirty companies approached in this stage were all in *The Times 100* 1969-70 largest British manufacturing enterprises. In addition, only private secretaries to managing directors who had had at least five years' experience and had held their current posts for at least six months were studied. This was to ensure that private secretaries had adapted to their bosses and organizations, and had developed a 'routine' for managing their jobs. The design of the sample is shown in Table 8.1.

The thirty private secretaries studied in the final stage were contacted via a letter from which an interview was arranged. The interview served to brief the secretary on the background to the project;

Table 8.1   *Design of sample by type of products*

| Types of products | Total number of companies | Number in sample |
|---|---|---|
| Tobacco | 1 | 1 |
| Metals and materials | 6 | 2 |
| Food | 6 | 5 |
| Oil | 4 | 3 |
| Power machinery | 5 | 3 |
| Chemicals | 5 | 4 |
| Pharmaceuticals and toiletries | 1 | 1 |
| Engineering | 10 | 4 |
| Textiles | 2 | 1 |
| Paper | 6 | 2 |
| Other | 4 | 4 |
| *Total* | 50 | 30 |

this was consciously kept quite vague so as not to sensitize the subjects to the area of activity actually being focused on in the research. In addition, the interview was used to acquire career background, a description of the structure of the organization, and how the secretary perceived her role within it. The main thrust of the interview was, however, geared to investigating the secretary's style of managing her boss's communication system. By picking up cues from the secretary I was able to investigate her actions in specific contexts. These covered both those occurring on a routine basis as well as the more exceptional situations where she (the secretary) saw herself having a lot of responsibility. It should be noted that I tended to use words like 'responsibility' and 'flexibility' rather than 'power' and 'influence' because of the emotive aspects attached to the latter words. The interview usually lasted between two and three hours.

On completion of the interview I left a package of documents for the secretary to fill in and return by post. These consisted of:

1 A Likert-type scale consisting of forty-eight statements describing a secretary's activities. The individual was asked to respond to this Likert-type scale, both in terms of her idea of an effective private secretary, and as a description of her own activities.
2 A diagnostic instrument measuring a number of key indices of the private secretary's behaviour. This investigated the degree to which she 'gatekeeps' the boss's diary, visitors, telephone calls, and mail; the size of each of these areas; as well as the specific patterns of actions she evolved within each of them.

3 An in-basket exercise aimed at eliciting a full description of how the private secretary reacted to a set of 'typical' work situations. These fifteen situations were compiled from the results of the early field-work.

The results of the interviews and the three instruments described above are covered in Chapters 4 to 6 of this book.

Figure 8.1 attempts to identify the three stages of the fieldwork described in this chapter and to integrate them into the whole framework of the actual development of the research. It is worth emphasizing here that the study did not progress in the tidy, discrete steps reflected in the chapter structure of this book, rather it was much more a process of zigzagging between conceptual thinking on the subject, and observation of the subject in the field. Although this strategy was probably more time-consuming than adopting a traditional approach of developing a set of theoretical hypotheses, testing them, and then interpreting them, I think it did help me to avoid distorting my observations in order for them to fit the theory neatly, or to bend the theory to match my observations. It is, perhaps, worth illustrating this point with three examples. Fiore suggests that the mix of a secretary's activities is solely determined by the personal needs of the private secretary.[4] This, however, does not reflect the situation of the secretaries I interviewed. All of them emphasized the importance of taking the lead from the boss's managerial style. This means that it is the boss who primarily determines the activities of his secretary, albeit that she may have considerable discretion in performing her role. The types of tasks that she will initiate will no doubt go some way in reflecting her personal work needs, as Fiore suggests, but by no means to the same extent.

A number of authors, notably Kanter, highlight the vicarious existence of the secretary in the organization. Kanter draws a close parallel between the boss's private secretary and his wife in terms of the dependency relationship. Further, the dependence of the secretary on the boss apparently explains the powerlessness of secretaries in organizations.[5] Again, the powerlessness of secretaries through their dependence on their bosses is by no means applicable to all secretaries in organizations. As I pointed out in Chapter 1, one of the main ways of differentiating the boss-secretary relationship up through the hierarchy is in terms of the changing dependency of one upon the other. At the top of the organizations I studied, it was the bosses who were dependent on their private secretaries, rather than vice versa. Further, once secretaries perceive this situation to exist, they have an

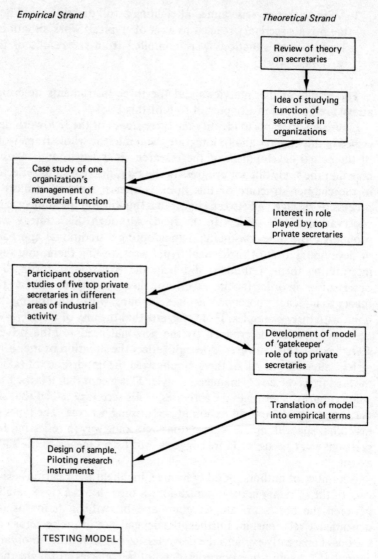

**Fig 8.1** *Development of the research study*

important power base on which to operate. This view is much more in keeping with Mechanic's theory on the power of lower participants in organizations.[6]

The third and last example to illustrate the gap between theory and observations on private secretaries, is related to the gatekeeper role. Most of the research to date on studying various types of gatekeepers in organizations stresses the significance of the role in terms of its ability to withhold or distort information.[7] While this also applies to private secretaries, another crucial element of their role, in my view, is their ability and regular practice of altering the timing and resequencing of information to their bosses. In other words, in a number of cases private secretaries may not alter the contents of communications to their bosses in a strict sense, but they may affect their timing and order of presentation. Thus, when analysing the private secretary as a gatekeeper in her boss's communication structure, it is necessary to look not only at *how* she processes communications, but also at the *priorities* she allocates to them when feeding them through to her boss.

These three minor examples illustrate the need I saw to examine theory critically at an early stage in the enquiry in order to evolve a useful and realistic perspective in my own research study (Figure 8.1).

# References and Notes

**Chapter 1**
1 Author unknown. 'The Secretarial Route to Success', *Business Management*, June 1971, p.33.
2 Thackray, J., 'The Secret of Secretaries', *Management Today*, April 1972, p.95.
3 Bain, G.S., and Price, R., 'Union Growth Revisited: 1948-1974 in Perspective', Mimeo, 1976, *British Journal of Industrial Relations*, vol. XIV, no. 3, pp.339-55.
4 Crozier, M., *The World of the Office Worker*, Chicago, University of Chicago Press, 1971, p.1.
5 Mills, C.W., as quoted by Silverman, D., 'Clerical Ideologies: a Research Note', *British Journal of Sociology*, vol. 19, 1968, p.326.
6 Bain, G.S., and Price, R., 'Who Is a White Collar Employee?', *British Journal of Industrial Relations*, vol. X, no. 3, 1972, pp.325-39.
7 Mills, C.W., *White Collar*, New York, Oxford University Press, 1951.
8 Lockwood, D., *The Blackcoated Worker*, London, Allen & Unwin, 1958.
9 Elliot, R.F., 'The Growth of White Collar Employment in Great Britain, 1951-1971', *British Journal of Industrial Relations*, vol. XV, no. 1, 1977, pp.39-44.
10 Parsons, T., *Structure and Process in Modern Societies*, Glencoe, Illinois, The Free Press, 1960.

11 Child, J., 'Parkinson's Progress: Accounting for the Number of Specialists in Organisations', *Administrative Science Quarterly*, vol. 18, no. 3, 1973, pp.328-48.
12 Downs, A., *Inside Bureaucracy*, Boston, Little, Brown & Co., 1969.
13 ibid.
14 Melman, S., 'The Rise of the Administrative Overhead in the Manufacturing Industries of the United States', Oxford, *Economic Papers*, 3, 1951, pp.6-112.
15 Parkinson, C., *Parkinson's Law and Other Studies in Administration*, Boston, Houghton Mifflin, 1957.
16 Rushing, W., 'Two Patterns of Industrial Administration', *Human Organisation*, vol. 26, nos. 1/2, Spring/Summer 1967, pp.32-9.
17 Tracy, L., 'Postscript to the Peter Principle', *Harvard Business Review*, July-August 1972.
18 Korda, M., *Power in the Office*, New York, Weidenfeld & Nicolson, 1976, pp.83-5.
19 Tracy, op. cit.
20 Lockwood, op. cit.
21 Braverman, H., *Labor and Monopoly Capital, the Degradation of Work in the Twentieth Century*, New York and London, Monthly Review Press, 1974, pp.293-358.
22 ibid.
23 Silverstone, R., 'The Office Secretary', unpublished Ph.D. thesis, University of London, 1974.
24 Shlakman, V., 'Status and Ideology of Clerical Workers', *Science and Society*, vol. XV, 1951, p.2.
25 Mills, op. cit.
26 Kanter, R.M., *Men and Women of the Corporation*, New York, Basic Books, 1977.
27 Census, England and Wales, 1971, Office of Population Censuses and Surveys, H.M.S.O., Occupational Table.
28 Bain and Price, 'Union Growth Revisited: 1948-1974 in Perspective', op. cit.
29 *Oxford English Dictionary*, vol. IX, Oxford, Clarendon Press, 1961.
30 Fiore, M., 'The Secretarial Role in Transition', *Supervisory Management*, November 1971, p.22.
31 Harwood, W., 'How to Get Rid of Your Most Attractive Status Symbol', *Financial Times*, 12 April 1972.
32 Berezin, E., 'How Technology is Freeing the Secretary', *Computers and Automation*, October 1972.
33 Kanter, op. cit., p.59.
34 Eccles, A., 'Wanted: Personal Manager, Preferably with Typing Skills', *Top Secretary*, May 1974, pp.44-5.
35 Roman, E., *The Secretary, Her Boss and Her Job*, London, Business Books, 1975, p.2.
36 Bensaher, J.G., 'The Guardian at the Office Door', *International Management*, January 1976.
37 Eccles, op. cit.
38 Goldhaber, G.M., 'Communication Audit of the Leon County System', Florida, unpublished, 1976.

39 Sorensen, B., 'The Professional Secretary: Key Asset of the Manager's Team', *The Business Quarterly*, vol. 39, no. 3, Autumn 1974.
40 MacKenzie, R., 'Are Executive Secretaries Obsolete?', *Personnel*, September 1971.

**Chapter 4**

1 Silverstone, R., 'The Office Secretary', unpublished Ph.D. thesis, University of London, 1974.
2 The reason for this was that pay tends to be more a reflection on the company's salary policy than an indication of individual performance. It would therefore be valuable to collect such data if comparing secretaries intra-organizationally, but not inter-organizationally, as was the case in this study.

**Chapter 5**

1 Handy, C.B., *Understanding Organisations*, Harmondsworth, Penguin, 1976, p.111.
2 Krech, D., Cruchfield, R., and Ballachey, E., *Individual in Society*, New York, McGraw-Hill, 1962, pp.226-46.

**Chapter 6**

1 Mintzberg, H., *The Nature of Managerial Work*, New York, Harper & Row, 1973, p.38.

**Appendix**

1 Campbell, D., and Fiske, D., 'Convergent and Discriminant Validation by the Multi-Trait-Multi-Method Matrix', *Psychological Bulletin*, vol. 56, 1959, pp.81-105.
2 Bruyn, S., *The Human Perspective in Sociology*, New Jersey, Prentice-Hall, 1966, p.15.
3 Silverman, D., *et al.*, *New Directions in Sociological Theory*, London, Collier Macmillan, 1972, p.192.
4 Fiore, M., 'The Secretarial Role in Transition', *Supervisory Management*, November 1971, p.22.
5 Kanter, R.M., *Men and Women of the Corporation*, New York, Basic Books, 1977.
6 Mechanic, D., 'Sources of Power of Lower Participants in Complex Organisations', *Administrative Science Quarterly*, 7, 1962, pp.349-64.
7 See for example, Allen, T., 'Meeting the Technical Information Needs of Research and Development Projects', Working Paper, Massachusetts Institute of Technology, Sloan School of Management, 1969. Pettigrew, A., 'Information Control as a Power Resource', *Sociology*, 1972, pp.187-204.

# Index

*In this index the letter-by-letter system has been adopted and feminine includes masculine. The word 'boss' rather than employer has been preferred since they are not necessarily synonymous. It should also be remembered that bosses are not necessarily masculine.*

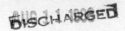